# Spiritual
# Kaizen

改善

GRANT HAGIYA

How to
Become
a Better Church Leader

Abingdon Press
*Nashville*

SPIRITUAL KAIZEN
HOW TO BECOME A BETTER CHURCH LEADER

**Library of Congress Cataloging-in-Publication Data**

Hagiya, Grant.
  Spiritual kaizen : how to become a better church leader / Grant Hagiya.
    pages  cm
  ISBN 978-1-4267-5322-0 (book - pbk. / trade pbk. : alk. paper)   1. Christian leadership—United Methodist Church (U.S.)   I. Title.
  BX8349.L43.H34 2013
  253—dc23

                                                                2012044345

"Focus-Energy Matrix" diagram on page 95 is from "Beware the Busy Manager," *Harvard Business Review*, Feb. 2, 2002.

"Life Cycle of a Church" diagram on page 117 is from *Leading Turnaround Churches* by Gene Wood. Reproduced with permission.

Manufactured in the United States of America

13 14 15 16 17 18 19 20 21 22—10 9 8 7 6 5 4 3 2 1

# CONTENTS

*To my Dad,*
*Moses K. Hagiya,*
*the greatest leader I have ever known*

# PREFACE

This is a book born out of three passions: my love of the church of Jesus Christ, my lifelong study in the Eastern martial arts, and my more recent study of leader and organizational development. This book weaves strands of these three life influences throughout, and what I have learned from all three.

Starting with the most foundational, I have been shaped and formed by the church of Jesus Christ. I was baptized as an infant, and my parents made the decision to bring my sister and me to Sunday school every week. When we moved to California from the city of my birth, Chicago, Illinois, we settled in a small farming community called San Jose. This was before Silicon Valley and the immense growth of the city. My parents found a Japanese American Christian church named Wesley United Methodist Church, and I attended every week from the age of six.

To say that this church had a profound influence on my faith life is an understatement. The church was constantly there for us through the difficulties of life, and when, at the age of fifteen, I lost my mom, the church enabled me to see a way forward and solidified my core belief in the Triune God. The church also encouraged my own leadership, allowing me to teach Sunday school and lead the youth group while still a young person myself. I taught Sunday school as a junior high schooler, and then I led the youth group during my high school and college years. These leadership opportunities were foundational for my own personal development, and the church gave more to me than I was able to give back.

The second strand of influence began when I was finishing grade school and entering junior high. I was fascinated by the martial arts. I read and practiced from every book on it in the local library, and finally started taking formal lessons at the age of thirteen. Martial arts started as a hobby for me but consumed my life in terms of experiences and lessons learned. I

vii

worked my way through the colored belt rankings and grew more and more interested in the art. I started teaching at my dojo (studio) in high school, and my teaching paid for most of my college education. I achieved the rank of Sandan (third-degree black belt) in Chinese Kenpo karate and branched out into other forms of Gung-fu styles through the years. I learned a great deal about leadership, especially from an Eastern perspective, through such martial arts training. One of the key characteristics that the martial arts developed for me was that of discipline. To master any art, one must develop the discipline of learning and application. In many of the Eastern arts, one learns the essence of the art through the practice of the form of the art itself. In the study and practice of the techniques of karate, I was able to grasp the Zen spirit philosophy of the inner art. As a beginner and intermediate student one simply attempts to perfect the physical techniques of karate, but in the advanced study of the art, one intuitively grasps the inner meaning of the core philosophy. Without mastery of the inner essence of karate, the techniques prove meaningless. I am forever grateful for this learned discipline, and readers will note the various points when I reflect upon my martial arts training as applied to leadership theory and practice.

Finally, for the past fifteen years, I have been turning to the secular world for leadership wisdom, and this culminated in my enrollment at a school that has faith-based roots, Pepperdine University, but whose curriculum comes from a secular organizational development perspective. At Pepperdine I pursued an EdD degree in organizational leadership. It was a wonderful learning experience, and I was the only faith-based professional in our cohort. Most of my papers were written on my work in the United Methodist Church, and at the time of my study I was a district superintendent overseeing the Los Angeles region of the Southern California area. My ultimate hope was to apply secular leadership and organizational development theory to the mainline church, and in the course of my studies, I attempted to do that very thing. My vision was to become an organizational consultant for the mainline church, as the cost of secular corporate consultants was out of the price range of most churches and judicatories. I wrote my dissertation on the traits, characteristics, and qualities of highly effective United Methodist Church clergy. It was a quantitative and qualitative study (mixed methods) that compared highly effective with less effective UMC clergy. This book is based on the research of my dissertation, as my hope is to translate some of my research findings to help church leaders refine their leadership approaches and practices.

Along my professional journey, the old Jewish saying came into play:

"Humans plan—God laughs." After completion of my coursework and comprehensives, I was elected a bishop of the United Methodist Church and became consumed by the responsibilities of oversight of the Pacific Northwest and Alaska Annual Conferences of the United Methodist Church.

After a short leave of absence from Pepperdine, when the learning curve was the highest in my new role and responsibilities as a bishop, I returned to my research and writing of the dissertation. It was always a stretch to work on a dissertation amidst such a demanding job, but by the grace of God, I managed to finish the dissertation and graduate in the winter of 2011. Also by the grace of God, the two annual conferences that I serve did not diminish or collapse during this crazy time of my life!

The discipline that I learned in my martial arts training helped me navigate the demands of finishing the degree while working more than full time. The intersection of all three of these strands contributes to the title and operating principle of this book, *Kaizen*, which means "steady and continuous growth and learning." I have spent a lifetime on my own faith journey, and my faith informs the basis of who I am and to whom I belong. Likewise, my martial arts training has provided a lifelong learning process, and every technique, experience, and style of martial art that I have studied has provided a slow and continuous sense of mastery of the art. Finally, my more recent study of leadership and organizational development has provided a basis for me to think and reflect on leadership and organizations in terms of systems and processes.

Finishing a dissertation and writing a book manuscript on my research findings while meeting the demands of an impossible job are a direct testimony to the kaizen concept. I wrote and researched about an hour a day on these two projects, setting aside this valuable time to concentrate. My ingrained sense of discipline enabled me to focus and prioritize this time to complete such tasks. However, concentrated work for one hour a day is not much of a sacrifice. Setting aside one hour each day really is not that major of a commitment. When I added up the cumulative hours, I again realized the effectiveness of the kaizen concept. Working one hour a day, every single day (and I mean every single day!), added up to forty-six eight-hour days. Imagine what you can accomplish with forty-six working days! The slow and continuous improvement of kaizen means that we can accomplish great things.

There are so many people to thank in regard to this book. First, I need to thank my family for their support and love. Next, I need to thank

the Pacific Northwest and Alaska Annual Conferences for allowing me the time to research and write. My Abingdon editor, Len Wilson, is a creative master, and it was Len who came up with the title of the book. I owe a great debt to early readers and reflectors Patricia Farris, Lee Hayward, and Greg Jones. I need to thank super laywoman Nancy Price for some early editing. I am indebted to my Administrative Assistant, Gretchen Engle for editing and proofreading, and for those who picked up the late editorial changes: Constance Stella and Jennifer Rogers, who are consummate professionals. All of you in your own way helped make this book possible.

Finally, I need to thank all of the rank-and-file clergy who serve our church with dedication and faithfulness. Oftentimes, they toil at their craft unnoticed; and yet with the principle of kaizen, lives are transformed and communities are made into better places to live. I pray that this book will increase their abilities to make a positive difference right where they live.

Grant Hagiya
Seattle, WA

CHAPTER 1

# Spiritual
# Leadership 101

*Knowledge is happiness, because to have knowledge—broad, deep
knowledge—is to know true ends from false, and lofty things from low.*
—Helen Keller
Author and lecturer

## The Unremarkable Pastor

He was a mid-career pastor with an unremarkable history. Neither great nor ineffective, his past service record demonstrated maintenance of local churches at which he served. From year to year there were slight fluctuations in worship attendance and membership statistics but no remarkable losses or gains.

Educated in a mainline Protestant seminary, he was trained in the basics of a standard theological degree: the formal disciplines of theology, biblical studies, church history, and ethics, and the practical arts of ministry—preaching, worship leadership, pastoral care and counseling, Christian education, and church administration. Because of the stability of society and church life at this time, there was a "cookie cutter" approach to preparing clergy for their careers. The prevailing pedagogy of almost all seminaries of his time was to provide a generalist degree program, touching briefly on all the basic subjects, and to produce a pastor who could step into almost any church and provide the basic programs for ministering to its congregation.

1

He was an average student while at seminary, progressing through the required curriculum, interning at a local church as a youth worker, and graduating with a Master of Divinity degree. He was neither at the top of his class nor at the bottom, a pattern that would follow him in the first four churches that he served.

To his judicatory supervisors, everything in his file and past service record pointed to "average, nondescript, unremarkable." The average tenure of his appointments at local churches was also fairly standard: four to six years at each local church he served. Now, facing the possibility of a fifth move, his judicatory supervisor, in consultation with colleagues and the bishop, proposed a lateral move. His reputation as "average" meant he was not going to hurt another church, but his gifts and graces did not suggest a promotion to a larger church, either.

Thus, these judicatory leaders, following a more subjective pathway rather than objective data, decided to move this pastor to a church about the same size as the one he currently served. The pastor at the new location was retiring, and the congregation had requested a replacement with experience rather than someone right out of seminary.

There was one important difference between the pastor's current church assignment and this new one: the demographics of the surrounding neighborhood of the new church were rapidly changing, and a new, large housing development was being completed that would attract thousands of first-time homebuyers and young families.

Unfortunately, this change in demographics was not the main driving force in the judicatory leadership's decision to assign the replacement pastor. Because the church was a small to average size congregation (an average of ninety in worship attendance), the appointment was not given a great deal of time and attention. The change was more a matter of expediency than strategic placement.

During this period there was also a huge outpouring of research and information on church growth and development of local congregations. Books, seminars, and workshops on the subject exploded on the church scene. This information was both inexpensive and accessible, and almost any pastor and congregation could immerse themselves in the literature.

The unremarkable pastor began to read and study the new information. As he learned, he became more and more excited and passionate about the concepts of church growth. Knowing that he would be taking on a new

church assignment, he committed to remaking himself and his ministry. He studied the literature and best practices. He attended every local seminar and workshop and even traveled to other well-known training events outside the area.

Because demographic analysis was a key strategy in congregational renewal, he studied the population reports and projections for his new church's surrounding community. He learned of the new housing development and that young families would be moving into the area of the church. Realizing the potential of a younger demographic, the pastor made plans based on this information and projected new outreach programs designed to attract these age groups.

Because not much was expected of the congregation, it was off the radar screen of the denomination. This reduced pressure on the pastor and gave him considerable flexibility to try new things. He began to experiment, trying out new church growth ideas and programs. As expected, some of them did not work, but others were successful. The congregation began to grow, slowly at first; but with each new concept or program, more people started visiting and participating.

Far from making random or arbitrary decisions about how to increase growth, the pastor learned in real time that there must be a systematic foundation for the church's growth. Again, from both the research and best practices and his own application of the information, he developed a fundamental plan based on four key systems: welcoming, discipling, outreach, and leadership development.

At first, the laity of the church reacted passively to their pastor's new directions and passion for growth. However, over time, as he enlisted more and more key lay leaders in new ministry pathways, new directions became contagious. Workshops and seminar sponsors asked that the church send ministry teams to the events. The pastor learned that if he could get 20 percent of the laity committed to a specific church strategy, their passion would pull the rest of the church forward. A paradigm shift took place in  his ministry. He realized that in the past he had seen himself as the sole leadership voice of the congregation, sometimes "bottlenecking" decisions and actions. Now he saw his job as empowering the laity to carry out the work of ministry. This proved to be a huge personal realization about his past ministry. If the church were to grow past a "pastoral size" (approximately 150 in worship attendance), he would have to empower the laity to take authority and responsibility. Over the next three years, as the laity took on more of

the ministry, the congregation grew to the "program size" (more than two hundred in worship attendance).

The pastor also realized that his learning curve had to continue rising to push beyond the two-hundred-in-worship attendance plateau. He had to reinvent himself and his leadership to reach the "corporate level" (more than 350 in worship attendance). He continued to study new church growth models, and he learned and grew.

He was allowed to stay in this appointment for a long term (sixteen years as he neared retirement), and this helped sustain the church's growth. By not moving this pastor, his supervisors enabled his new skills to develop. Combined with an energized laity whose social context the pastor understood and a positive demographic, the church continued in growth and vitality.

When the judicatory leaders began to recognize the new skill sets of this pastor, they asked him to move to even larger local churches a couple of times. He wisely resisted and retired as the beloved pastor of the church. After more than twenty-four years of ministry, the pastor had seen his church's attendance more than triple to become one of the strongest and most vibrant in that district.

There is much to be learned from this particular story, but let's start with the most obvious: how is it that an average local church pastor can turn into a highly effective and growth-oriented pastor? Obviously, he was not born with innate leadership skills that suddenly kicked in when he reached middle age. Nor was there some dramatic event in the pastor's life or the life of the congregation that catapulted the church into a period of accelerated growth.

While a lot of interlocking factors aided the success of this pastor and his local church, the premise of this book is that leadership traits are not set at birth and that all of us can grow and develop into more effective leaders at any time during our careers. In the following chapters I work from both secular and ecclesial models of leadership, comparing and contrasting the two, in order to draw out the best leadership models available for current and future leaders of the church.

# Spiritual Leadership Kaizen: Continuous Improvement

The title of this book applies a Japanese business practice to the spiritual leadership of clergy and laity. The Japanese word *kaizen* derives from the root words *kai*, translated in English as "change," and *zen*, translated as "good" or "better." The concept that Japanese management created was

4

"continuous improvement," and major companies such as Toyota Motors developed a management philosophy that enabled them to become highly successful worldwide leaders in their business area. Such Japanese companies believe in steady and continuous improvement over time rather than big, flashy innovations.

As I hope to apply it to your personal spiritual leadership, spiritual kaizen means slow, steady, yet continuous improvement. In practical terms it means that every day I learn one new thing, work on improving one behavior, or try to apply one new skill set. It means an intentional focus on a specific leadership learning, behavior, or practice. It also involves evaluative self-reflection. Such practices do not have to involve huge, ambitious, drastic changes or objectives but rather require small, incremental, positive ones. If every day I learn, grow, or develop in my leadership capacity, over time I make a huge leap.

I wish I had known about the concept of kaizen on my own spiritual journey. I was ordained a deacon in the former two-step United Methodist process as a twenty-four-year-old student who was only halfway through seminary. With my limited understanding of John Wesley's doctrine, I was greatly troubled by his conception that spiritual perfection was attainable. I was fine with the spiritual movement from justification to sanctification and truly believed that I would continue to work on my spiritual life in this process. However, I had trouble believing that anyone could attain the state of spiritual perfection that he called "entire sanctification." Personally, I was just too flawed a human being, and my study of history pointed to the only empirically verifiable Christian doctrine: sin!

I was to be ordained at my United Methodist annual conference—the first time I had ever been to an annual conference! We ordination candidates were briefed that the bishop would read the classical examination questions from John Wesley, and we were to answer our affirmations in a loud and enthusiastic voice. We went over the questions and there was the dreaded question about perfection: "Are you going on to perfection?" I was okay with all of the other questions, including an embarrassing one about not being in debt. But how could I answer that question when I really didn't believe I could attain such perfection? When the time came for the historical questions, I was going to say "no" but chickened out at the last minute and merely remained silent as my ordination colleagues answered "yes."

Since that time I have come to understand Wesley in a deeper way, and the concept of kaizen has helped that understanding. If I intentionally grow

in my love of God and neighbor a little bit more each and every day, then I am going on to a form of perfection. It is much like the Mahayana Buddhist concept of *satori,* or enlightenment, in which attaining such a state in a momentary occasion in this earthly life is possible, but maintaining it is elusive. However, intentional and daily practice of the spiritual disciplines (Wesley called them "the means of grace") will provide the grounding for continuous spiritual improvement.

I firmly believe that any spiritual leader who does not practice spiritual kaizen, or the observation of daily spiritual disciplines, cannot remain effective very long. The rigors of ministry are just too intense to survive without a regular connection with God and the spiritual replenishing that follows. Spiritual kaizen is absolutely essential if we are to grow as spiritual leaders.

# The Secular Leadership Literature

Leadership literature is not very old as academic disciplines go, and it began with the more focused examination of leadership traits. The earliest psychological study of leaders, attributed to the pioneer Lewis Terman, focused on the personality traits or qualities of individual leaders. Originally dubbed the "Great Man" approach, it was the foundation for leadership studies. This theory reached its height of popularity between the 1940s and 1960s, and is still used to assert that leaders become effective by utilizing their innate abilities. "Traits are considered to be patterns of individual attributes, such as skills, values, needs, and behaviors, which are relatively stable in the sense that they tend to repeat over time."[1] The most common traits associated with this leadership style are intelligence, self-confidence, determination, integrity, and sociability.[2] Such abilities are characterized by attributes that set people apart from their organizational counterparts or peers: educational levels, physical health, social standing and upbringing, communication capacity, cognitive ability, masculinity, decision-making aptitude, and what is now known as emotional intelligence.

The original foundation of the "Great Man" theory of leadership shows its sexism in the misguided assertion that individuals are born with innate traits that make them great leaders. Modern research has pretty much debunked the idea that leaders are born, not made, but the general public continues to cling to this myth.

The church is not immune to this lack of enlightenment. In fact, theologically, the "Savior-Hero" complex of the Christian tradition reinforces the "Great Man" theory of leadership.

Because of post-critical atonement theories of Jesus' soteriological significance (his saving power), many Christians still relate to Christ through his saving power alone. There is no doubt in my mind that I am saved through the power of Jesus' grace. However, the complexity of Jesus underscores how much we can truly learn from him. Here, Christology, or the study of who Jesus was, is critical to the theme of leadership.

As I study the Gospel reflections of Jesus, there is a strong case that he rejected the opportunity to become the earthly savior-leader of a worldly political movement. He consistently let down those who wanted a political messiah to liberate them from Roman domination and oppression.

A key example comes from the Gospel of John's account of the feeding of the five thousand. In John's account, Jesus takes more initiative as compared with the Synoptic stories of the same event. However, it is the concluding verse fifteen that draws our attention: "When Jesus realized that they were about to come and take him by force to make him king, he withdrew again to the mountain by himself" (John 6:15).

There is no question that Jesus has fulfilled one of the prime characteristics of true leadership: he has followers, and these followers wish to give him power over them. As biblical scholars Bruce Malina and Richard Rohrbaugh comment on the nature of "kingship," "Kings are not simply a political equivalent of a 'president' with rights of hereditary succession. Rather, kings have total control of and responsibility for their subjects; they are expected to provide them with fertility, peace and abundance."[3]

That the people believe in Jesus so much that they wish to actually force him to become their king is telling. In his earthly ministry he rejects the savior-hero complex that the people wish to thrust upon him. Later, in John 18:36, he declares that the only kingdom he seeks is a spiritual one, not an earthly one. However, it is not a stretch to project onto Jesus his intuitive understanding that dabbling in any earthly power will eventually let the people down. His mission from God was not one of earthly power and political domination, so he withdraws alone away from the crowds to escape their misguided intentions.

## Jesus: What Kind of Leader?

So, if Jesus rejected the role of worldly political leader, what kind of leader was he? I believe he was the ultimate model of "spiritual leader" and so remains for us the prime example of how to lead in the church. In this sense, he was teaching us how to learn, and he continues to teach us, as we

are led by the Holy Spirit, to deal with new situations and contexts in the present.

Take for example his interaction with the disciples in their quest for more power and recognition as reported in Mark 10:35–45. The brothers James and John ask Jesus a loaded question: "Teacher, we want you to do for us whatever we ask of you" (v. 35). Jesus responds with a simple question: "What is it you want me to do for you?" (v. 36).

The brothers wish to be elevated above the other disciples and sit at the place of honor on Jesus' right and left side. Jesus responds as a true leader by defining reality for James and John: "You do not know what you are asking. Are you able to drink the cup that I drink, or be baptized with the baptism that I am baptized with?" (v. 38). In other words, are you willing to follow God's will to die with me? Foolishly, they answer, "We are able" (v. 39).

Instead of demoralizing them and questioning their abilities, Jesus graciously affirms them by acknowledging that they will follow him down the path of costly discipleship that leads to eternal life. However, once again, he refuses to play the role of savior-hero and in honesty tells them that he does not have the power to grant their request.

Naturally, when the rest of the disciples hear about what James and John have asked for, they become indignant and jealous. After all, James and John are seeking recognition out of their own self-interest and ambition, and this spreads the deadly disease of factionalism within any team. It divides and alienates teammates from one another.

Jesus' leadership is immediate: he calls them all together to teach them.

> You know that those who are considered rulers over the Gentiles lord it over them, and their great ones exercise authority over them. Yet it shall not be so among you; but whoever desires to become great among you shall be your servant. And whoever of you desires to be first shall be slave of all. For even the Son of Man did not come to be served, but to serve, and to give His life a ransom for many. (vv. 42-5 NKJV)

Jesus knows he must defuse their anger and division, so he starts his talk by pointing out how negatively the secular world handles power and ambition. But then comes his affirmation and belief in them: "But it is not so among you." This is followed by an even deeper spiritual truth as compared to the world: To be great, one must first serve, not be served, and to be first, one must model as a slave to all.

8

Then Jesus consummates his teaching by putting himself on the line: he has come not to be served, but to serve, and to give his own life as a ransom for all. Do the disciples understand what he is really saying? Probably not. The fullness of this teaching moment will not come to them until after his crucifixion and resurrection. However, will they remember this teaching moment after he has modeled the physical sacrifice of his own life for them and the whole world? Of course they will.

The modeling of leadership by Jesus in this passage is remarkable by today's standards. In this one conversation, he moves in and out of different styles of leadership to be effective. Let's take a closer look at how Jesus leads.

First, to James and John's ridiculously loaded statement, "Teacher, we want you to do for us whatever we ask of you" (v. 35), Jesus is not defensive or sarcastic. In what appears to be a non-anxious state of mind, he responds: "What is it you want me to do for you?" (v. 36).

When their request comes in a very self-centered and divisive form, Jesus once again does not react with anger or contempt but attempts to teach them by enabling them to see the true reality of what they are asking. Are they willing to go through everything that God asks of Jesus? Are they really willing to die a horrible and lonely death as he will? Being full of themselves, they say, "Of course we can do that."

Jesus' style shifts again to one of collaboration and encouragement, so his response accepts that they will follow him to death and beyond. But he also tells them honestly that he does not have the power to grant them what they are asking and thereby shifts to an adaptive leadership style.

Following this conversation, the rest of Jesus' team gets very upset, and Jesus shifts to a more directive style by gathering all of the disciples together and teaching them. It reminds me of a great manager-leader of a sports team who delivers that stirring motivational talk to get the team to perform beyond its capabilities. At the end Jesus personalizes it by reminding them of his own commitment to God on behalf of all humanity.

# Six Styles of Leadership

When we speak of "styles" of leadership, we usually assume that people are locked into a specific style and do not deviate from it. Examples include: "He has a very directive, authoritarian style," or "she has a very collaborative and relational style." But effective leadership means that one should change styles in order to match the context of the situation one faces. Daniel

9

Goleman is one of the strongest advocates of this "situational model" of leadership. From the Hay-McBer study, Goleman identifies six distinct styles of leadership:

- Coercive
- Authoritative
- Affiliative
- Democratic
- Pacesetting
- Coaching[4]

Let's take a quick look at the different styles by starting with the coercive style (Goleman later changed the name to commanding), which is top down and demands immediate compliance. It is a disciplinary style that is hierarchical and commanding. It tends to get short-term, immediate results, but because of its negativity turns workers off and has few long-term motivational effects. The coercive style does result in some success in times of crisis or immediate turnaround situations.

The authoritative style (a somewhat misleading name) wishes to mobilize people toward a vision. Instead of being demanding of others, it attempts to invite them to join a positive direction or vision. The emphasis is placed on a communal or organizational goal rather than individual achievement. It naturally works best in a change-of-management situation or when a clear direction is called for.

The affiliative style is the most relational of the six. It attempts to create harmony and build emotional bonds between people. It is a people-first style that takes personal interest in workers and is genuinely concerned with their welfare. Obviously, the style centers on relationship building and communication. It is a strong style for building team harmony and strengthening morale when there has been a breakdown in trust and honesty.

The democratic style is perfectly named in that it attempts to build consensus through direct participation. It is a collaborative style that asks workers for their opinions and attempts to get "buy-in" from as large a segment of the organization as possible. This style tends to build morale, participation, and empowerment and in general has a positive outcome for most organizations. It works best when the leader or organization is uncertain about what to do or where to go next in the near future.

The pacesetting style is a high-accountability model that sets a very high bar and asks everyone to aspire to such a bar. It is a high-achiever's model that asks and demands the very best effort and work from its employees and sets measurements to assess if one is achieving such goals. People who use this style tend to lead by example and must model the high performance that they are asking of others. Ironically, over time, it tends to harm morale and motivation rather than improve it. Often employees feel overwhelmed with the demands and their inability to meet increasingly high expectations. This style works best with a high-performing, self-motivated individual or team with high self-esteem.

Finally, the coaching style is what the name implies: a developmental approach that is most concerned with building leadership for the future. Like good coaching, it centers on the individual and attempts to develop that individual to the best of his or her abilities. Good coaching helps individuals improve on their strengths and address their weaknesses, sets goals and directions, and enables individuals to be held accountable for what they have established as objectives. It is a positive approach to long-term leadership development, but it is the least-used style due to the need for immediate results and the pressures of most organizations' competitive environments. This style works best when employees are motivated to improve their skills and performance and when the organization has the luxury of time and resources to develop future leaders.

The most helpful recommendation from Goleman is his observation that the most effective leaders use more than one style, or better yet, all six, depending on the specific situation that one faces. His analogy is an important one, which is to think of the styles as

> an array of clubs in a golf pro's bag. Over the course of a game, the pro picks and chooses clubs based on the demands of the shot. Sometimes he has to ponder his selection, but usually it is automatic. The pro senses the challenge ahead, swiftly pulls out the right tool, and elegantly puts it to work. That's how high-impact leaders operate, too.[5]

Most leaders change styles based on the specific situation they encounter, but as we have seen, in only one situation Jesus changes styles repeatedly in dealing with his own disciples. Thus Jesus exemplifies the effective leader that Goleman envisions, and so can each of us.

**11**

# Do This, Not That!

I want to be clear and prescriptive. It is important for spiritual leaders not to get locked into a specific style of leadership but to read the situation and context and apply the leadership style that would best match it. Because of the myriad of roles and situations that clergy encounter in the local church, we must constantly adapt our leadership to the present challenge that confronts us. Such situational leadership means that we must constantly read the present situation and then seek the best leadership style that will proactively address that particular context. Too often I have witnessed clergy who are locked into a specific style of leadership that they are comfortable with, and then they are unable to adapt to a constantly changing context in ministry. The perfect example is the "pastoral size" style, where the spiritual leader is the center of everything at the local church. In order to move out of the "family size" style of chaplaincy, the pastor is rewarded for growing a church to be the central hub of ministry. It produces a certain kind of success and affirmation. However, in moving to the "program size" style of resourcing the laity, the pastor cannot adapt from being the center of ministry to giving up direct leadership of everything that goes on in the church and fails to adapt to the next size transition. We will pick up this theme again and again in spiritual leadership, but the important thing to remember here is to use styles of leadership like different golf clubs in your ministry bag that are tailored for changing contexts.

# We Want a Savior-Hero to Lead Our Church

Just as the "Great Man" theory continues to live on in our secular world, so too the "Savior-Hero" model continues to thrive throughout our churches. From the top to the bottom of our denominational structures, it is hoped that such a savior will emerge. The church is desperate for such "super leadership," but is consistently let down when leaders do not match up to unrealistic expectations. No one can fulfill such expectations, and good leaders realize this intuitively. To paraphrase Harvard's Ron Heifetz and Marty Linksy, "Leadership is letting people down at a rate that they can tolerate."[6]

Adding to this problem is the growing secularity of our churches, which produces a "consumerism mentality." Instead of being true to the historic, biblical roots of an outward mission focus, of serving the needs of the lost and hurting in our midst, we resort to the church itself being the object of care and attention.

We bishops receive a steady stream of letters, and, of course, we get our share of complaints. The vast majority of the complaint letters reflect some dissatisfaction with the local church, and it is usually something that we cannot fix. However, when letters are received that complain about the system either taking away (a good complaint, in a way!) or replacing the pastor (much more negative), the theme of the letter is "Take care of me!" The congregation acts as a consumer who expects to receive a service, be it religious truth, pastoral care, meaning in life, or a way to cope with the rigors of daily living. When the church engages in this pay-for-fee service, it prostitutes itself to an attitude of give and take, quid pro quo, a transaction where the client expects value for his or her dollar.

The consumer mentality sees the congregation member as the client, where the responsibility of the church leader is to take care of the parishioner. In this consumerism model, leaders are evaluated on how well we take care of the client, and that client has a responsibility to fund and give volunteer time to make sure the church continues to exist.

To devolve into such a consumerism model reflects the depths of our human sin and our need for redemption. The church of Jesus Christ must consider its client to be God alone. Anything less dissolves into a selfish preoccupation with our own needs and wants. If God is our client, then our mission and purpose must revolve around that which God wishes. Biblically, that means an outward focus on the needs of the other, and especially for justice to the poor, the sojourner, and widow in our midst.

In terms of a leadership model, the mission of the church has never been a transactional one, in which something mutually beneficial is exchanged. Rather, our missional model is one of transformation, where both parties are lifted to a higher level of love of life.

For example, liberation theologian Juan Luis Segundo used the transactional model of the "economy of energy" principle in one analysis of Christ's ministry. In this model, Jesus only has a limited supply of human energy to give. When the crowds become so large and invasive, he can only give out so much energy and compassion. He must resort to removing himself and limiting what he can give. Segundo's point is that even Christ has limits to his energy and in a way practices a form of violence by withholding energy from those in need.[7]

It seems clear enough that Jesus struggled with how to minister to the crowds that became so large that he could not effectively help them all as individuals. However, I fundamentally disagree with the businesslike model

of the "economy of energy" to characterize Jesus. In a true model of adaptive leadership, Jesus changes tactics in his ministry by empowering his disciples to preach, teach, and heal individuals in the large crowds. He gives over his power from God to the disciples, who carry out his ministry. But it doesn't stop there. Somewhere in their leadership, the disciples realize that they cannot do it alone either. So, as recorded in the book of Acts, they create the church, and through baptism empower the believers to carry out the ministry that Jesus started. We are the heirs to this adaptive strategy. In baptism, we are empowered with the gifts of God to preach, teach, and heal the lost, lonely, and hurting in our world. All baptized Christians are so commissioned. There cannot be a consumer mentality in such a process. As baptized Christians we are not primarily to be taken care of, but through the gifts empowered to us by Jesus we must take care of others. This is what it means to be the Church of Jesus Christ.

Segundo's analysis also addresses the personal leadership style of Jesus. Consider John's account of the interaction of Jesus with the Samaritan woman at the well. The Samaritan woman keeps pressing for a transactional relationship with Jesus. Remember, she wants the living water that Jesus speaks of, and, like a true consumer, keeps asking where she can get this water. Jesus is equally insistent on making this a transformational relationship and keeps digging into the woman's life and history in order to mine the deeper levels of her self-actualization. In this short personal encounter, Jesus pushes past any crass transaction, and she goes away transformed with a commitment to God and the zeal to spread this news of God to her own community. Whereas Segundo's economy of energy principle speaks of the quantitative dimension of our ministry in Jesus' name, the John passage proclaims the qualitative dimension that sees no limits of energy or compassion. The business-consumer world is preoccupied with quantitative data in the form of zero-sum calculations, supply and demand, and winners and losers. The transformational power of Jesus puts its emphasis in the qualitative dimension that only comes from God: unlimited grace, infinite possibilities, and the deep well of the human soul that speaks to the fact that anyone can be changed and transformed through the power of the Triune God.

# A Developmental Model of Leadership

The Gallup StrengthsFinder literature has a helpful model for the basic question of innate versus learned leadership traits and qualities. They define

a "talent" as a more innate quality that cannot be learned. Their definition of talent is "a naturally recurring pattern of thought, feeling, or behavior that can be productively applied."[8] The best example of a talent for our purposes is agility, hand-eye coordination, or speed. You can enhance these God-given talents, but you are born with them for the most part. This goes back to the popular basketball quotation: "You can't teach height." In this case, you either have it, or you don't.

The Gallup folks distinguish talent from those elements that one can definitely work on and improve: skills, knowledge, and experience. One isn't born or hard-wired with these factors, but they can be acquired through time. Gallup defines skills as "the basic ability to move through the fundamental steps of a specific task."[9] We can learn the fundamentals of a specific skill, and then we can hone that skill through intensive practice and repetition. Shooting a basketball is the perfect example: there are basic fundamentals such as an L-shaped arm position, wrist cocked back for the release, and finger rotation off the seams of the ball as the wrist flicks forward with backspin on the ball. Practiced repetitively, one develops the skill set to effectively shoot a basketball.

Knowledge is another example of something that is learned over time. The Gallup literature defines knowledge as "what you know as a result of formal or informal education." Although there are some talents that enhance knowledge—high IQ, ability to recall facts, strong memory, and so on—knowledge is an acquired asset.

Experience is also not innate but rather something we develop over time. Experiences over time seem to enhance one's ability to deal with most contingencies. I once had a physician who introduced himself by saying that he had performed this one medical procedure that I was facing over two thousand times in his career. It was his way of assuring me that he had the experience to handle any problems that might arise unexpectedly. Obviously, most people prefer a medical doctor who has performed the same procedure two thousand times instead of two times.

The last element that one can acquire is the "fit" that one has in a role or job. Fit speaks more to the style one brings to a certain job or role, as in "She is a good 'fit' in our company," or "He is the perfect 'fit' for this role." Fitting in has a great deal to do with one's emotional intelligence and ability to adapt to new environments and circumstances.

The Gallup folks believe that the combination of all of these factors leads to a set of signature strengths that each person possesses. A strength

is defined as "the ability to consistently provide near-perfect performance in a specific task."[10] They believe that our strengths have been formed by the aforementioned elements, and the culmination of these results is a set of strengths.

The following diagram provides an illustration of all of these factors:

# STRENGTH

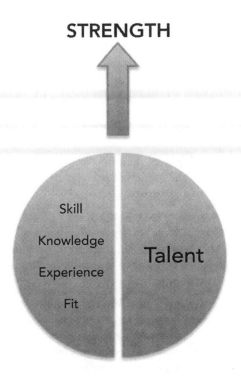

Skill

Knowledge

Experience

Talent

Fit

There is little doubt that talent plays a factor in our effectiveness in ministry, but equally important are the skills, knowledge, experience, and fit that we develop and acquire over time. This book focuses on the elements that we can learn and acquire, as all of us can become stronger spiritual leaders. This is also the reason that kaizen is such an important concept in leadership: if we dedicate ourselves to improving in small ways each and every day, then through our intentional growth experiences in ministry we build a stronger leadership base on a regular basis.

Much current research focuses on the fact that it takes around ten thousand hours to master an art, profession, or major skill set. This means

that if I practice five hours a day every single day of the year, it will take me about six years to gain a mastery level. More realistically, if I practice four hours a day, five days a week, it will take me around ten years to reach this level of practice time. Kaizen is about focused, steady improvement over ten or more years to reach such mastery. It is impossible to get it all at once, so we need to resort to the kaizen way in our leadership development.

## The Center of Creative Leadership's 70-20-10 Rule

The Center of Creative Leadership (CCL) is one of the premier secular leadership research centers in America. They recently published some of their research findings on what they call the "70-20-10 Rule." This rule applies to those leaders who learn and grow over the course of their careers. Their research is based on the same premise as this book, that leaders can learn and grow over the course of their careers. For CCL, leadership is learned. To quote the article, "We believe that today, even more than before, a manager's ability and willingness to learn from experience is the foundation for leading with impact."[11] Their guideline for experience is expressed in a ratio: 70 percent of that experience is in challenging assignments, 20 percent is found in developmental relationships, and only 10 percent is in coursework and training.

Clearly, challenging assignments forge the growth that makes the most difference in leader development, and their research points to three key experiences that cut across international business assignments: (1) managing direct reports (those personnel who report directly to you), (2) self-awareness, and (3) executing effectively.[12]

As we apply this to spiritual leaders, managing a staff of paid and volunteer workers is one of the biggest challenges for pastors coming out of seminary. Unless a pastor has had this type of management experience in another setting, there is usually a huge learning curve when it comes to supervising people.

As a young twenty-six-year-old pastor in my first full-time appointment, I was declared the senior pastor of a small church that also had a part-time Japanese-language pastor. This pastor was in his late sixties and had thirty years of experience on me, yet I was assigned as his senior. Talk about contradictions! We seemed to work well together the first couple of years, but as I got to know the situation, I felt he was not doing enough for the small group of Japanese elders that the church had as members. So

I had one of those "supervision" meetings with him. Remember, I was a young kid, and he had over thirty years of experience on me. Anyone could predict how badly such a meeting would go. But being young and naïve, I thought this was my role as senior pastor, and I really cared about these elderly members. If I had had even a tenth of the experience and knowledge I have now, I would have handled this situation completely differently, but as one might guess, the meeting did not go well. He was offended that I felt he was not doing enough (which was the truth), was insulted that I would think that of him, and immediately left in a huff to call the chairperson of the Staff-Parish Relations Committee (the lay personnel committee of the church). The chairperson immediately called me and told me of my associate's anger due to our supervision meeting, but agreed with my assessment that he was not doing very much for our Japanese-speaking members. I had the full confidence of this chairperson and the committee, so we worked out a way in which the committee itself could help hold the associate pastor accountable. I now see that I never should have met with the associate pastor by myself but should have used the Staff-Parish Relations Committee to do the direct supervision work. With much effort and collaboration, we helped the pastor to retire in the next year.

Such was my dramatic introduction to managing direct reports. Of course, I learned immensely from this experience and every other staff management role that I took from that point on. However, one of the steepest learning curves that younger pastors encounter is when they have to manage more direct reports than they ever have before. Moving to a large church (program or corporate size) means that the role of staff management becomes central to the senior pastor, and many clergy do not know how to supervise effectively. As I supervise senior pastors of large churches, this consistently seems like the hardest transition for them to make from smaller settings. These senior pastors often remark that their most challenging work comes from supervising staff.

The second area of self-awareness is a major premise of this book, and I explore that experience extensively when I address emotional intelligence. Suffice it to say I believe that self-awareness and self-knowledge is the most fundamental element of leadership success, and the lack of self-awareness is one of the highest contributors to failure in the ministry.

The final element of "executing effectively" seems painfully obvious. For growth to happen, one has to have success in execution. If there is one obvious quick win in the ministry or any other profession, it is to demonstrate effective execution of almost any program, event, or process in

the church. For example, the first funeral of a significant member of the congregation sets up the true test for a new pastor. In my Asian-American church tradition, it is the single most important litmus test of execution in the ministry. How one conducts and behaves during and in the follow-up to that very first funeral in the community is often the lens with which parishioners and community members judge a pastor. It sets the image and perception of a new pastor for years.

The problem with this issue of "executing effectively" lies in the lack of specific guides on how one does this. Obviously, it depends on what one is executing, and in the ministry, there are many variables that require performance. Funerals, weddings, public gatherings, invocations, worship, preaching, and special programs—the list goes on and on. In fact, there are probably very few professions that call upon such a diverse and varied set of roles and duties. In fact, Richard DeShon and Abigail Quinn, two Michigan State University researchers who studied the role of clergy, commented that they had never seen another profession where individuals had to switch roles so often and so quickly. They called this phenomenon "multitasking and polychronic orientation," and they were surprised at the sheer number of roles and duties that comes with pastoral ministry. As DeShon comments, "I have never encountered such a fast-paced job with such varied and impactful responsibilities."[13] As clergy we know intimately the almost schizophrenic pace of role change and sets of tasks that must be done in the course of any given day. It would do us well to be reminded how difficult the job of pastoring truly is and to acknowledge the complexities of polychronic role display.

One final comment regarding the high percentage (70 percent) attributed to growth in the form of actual challenging assignments: challenging assignments in the secular world usually mean more responsibilities, a higher tier of leadership role (executive level), and increased pay. These factors do not always compute well in the local church. Challenging local church assignments are growing in number, but that is because many of our churches are on the edge of survival in terms of finances and membership. These church assignments are challenging in the reverse direction not because they are growing and large but because they are diminishing and functioning in survival mode. The traditional career ladder for clergy—promotion to increasingly larger and more prestigious churches—is gone. We have a few large churches that are vital and growing, but the vast majority of United Methodist congregations are small to medium in size, and many of them are struggling. The following table gives the actual statistics of the high percentage of small membership churches.

## Small Membership Churches in the United Methodist Church

| Worship Attendance | No. of Churches | Percentage | Cumulative Percentage |
|---|---|---|---|
| 50 or fewer | 17,321 | 48.5% | 48.5% |
| 50-100 | 8,722 | 24.4% | 72.9% |
| 100-200 | 1,991 | 5.6% | 78.5% |

Data taken from the General Board of Global Ministries database, Rev. John Southwick.

The fact that 73 percent of all United Methodist congregations have one hundred people or fewer in worship will not undergird a system of clergy career advancement. The truth is that many clergy appointments are lateral, and we just don't have a lot of outstanding and growing churches to which we can promote our clergy.

So the real challenge for most clergy is to take a diminishing or dying church and make it vital and growing. Many of our churches are in "turn-around" mode, and the challenge is being able to create health and vitality in a diminishing setting.

However, if a pastor is not trained in the work of turning a church around, then instead of being challenged to produce growth, it turns into an overwhelming experience. The pastor has no clue where to start. This latter outcome is more the norm, and because clergy are not specifically trained in turnaround situations, the experience drains and demoralizes them instead of energizing and inspiring them.

So, the other two experiences that the Center for Creative Leadership posits are critical to helping clergy make it in a turnaround ministry: developmental relationships (20 percent) and coursework and training (10 percent).

Developmental relationships for clergy come in the form of supervisors, mentors, and coaches who work directly with clergy to support them in their challenging assignments. Most mainline judicatories do not provide the necessary support for clergy to help them serve at their best. Most judicatories are stretched too thin in terms of funding and resources to be of much help. The clergy who succeed in such challenges are usually those

who have tremendous natural gifts and abilities or those who marshal their own mentors, role models, or coaches to support them.

Many of us at the judicatory level are trying to change this paradigm by putting all of our resources in support of clergy and local churches in direct development, training, and coaching. In the United Methodist Annual Conference in which I serve, we have started the Bishop Jack and Marjorie Tuell Center of Leadership Excellence, after our beloved bishop couple in the Northwest. Both Jack and Marjorie exemplified excellence in their careers and were committed to the development of clergy and churches. Our center hopes to provide a three-prong approach by providing *development* to clergy and churches who need to grow in a new way of doing church, *training* in the form of actual skill-set teaching in turnaround and revitalization of churches, and *coaching* in the ongoing support of clergy.

Furthermore, all of the district superintendents (middle judicatory supervisors) and staff of the annual conference are being trained in their skill sets to be able to deliver to lay-clergy teams specific ways to grow and revitalize local churches. The district superintendents and staff are also being trained in their coaching skills, and a sustainable coaching model is being developed to provide coaching for those in need of such support.

In my dream world, every clergy member would have a performance coach in ministry, a spiritual director to enhance their faith journey, a therapist or counselor to reflect on their psyche, a trusted mentor to guide and impart wisdom, and a life coach to give them balance and harmony in both their professional and personal life. The cost of such support would be prohibitive for any judicatory, but clergy can provide such roles for each other. If we develop a deeper sense of communal accountability, we will find a way to provide such support for each other.

The vision that undergirds all of this is that through supportive developmental relationships and training, we can provide the tools for our clergy to grow in their challenging assignments. However, the big picture is the need for the entire system to be supportive of the growth of clergy and lay leadership. Of prime importance is the motivation of individuals to grow in their leadership of the church, but all the systems of the church must be posed to contribute to and support this growth.

# Do This, Not That!

Ministry is just too difficult and complex to go it alone. The "lone ranger" mentality will surely lead to burnout and ineffectiveness—if not

now then in the future of one's ministry. It is absolutely essential for clergy to develop relationships with supportive colleagues and networks like we have mentioned above.

You can go it alone for a short period of time, but the rigors of the ministry will catch up with you eventually. It is illustrative that Jesus' first priority was to call a team of disciples together to lead and, when it came time, send them off (in some Gospel accounts, two-by-two) to do the work of ministry. Do not go it alone, but develop the partnerships and networks that will sustain your ministry.

## The Nature of Leadership

One final thought when it comes to the focus of this book, namely leadership: I find any one definition of leadership totally inadequate to capture its essence. Leadership is just too large to be narrowed down to one specific definition. I agree with the adaptive leadership writers like Heifetz and Linsky, who see leadership as a verb, or something that one does. Certainly having followers, authority, and power play into the ability to lead, but in the end, these are only tools with which one can carry out leadership either effectively or poorly. In the end, leadership is best described as a verb, and as we act in effective leadership, we fulfill its great potential. It is for this reason that I will focus on the behaviors of spiritual leaders, as it underscores the reality that leadership is a verb.

As baptized Christians, all of us must exert our own leadership in the church and world. All of us have been given the powers of God to make a difference right where we live. Furthermore, each one of us can improve our leadership abilities on a continual, slow, and steady basis (kaizen), and in the pages that follow, I hope to show how to do this.

## For Further Reading: On General Leadership

Bolman, Lee, and Terrance Deal. *Reframing Organizations, Artistry, Choice and Leadership*. 3rd ed. San Francisco: Jossey-Bass, 2003.

Collins, Jim. *Good to Great*. New York: HarperCollins, 2001.

Collins, Jim, and Morton Hansen. *Great by Choice*. New York: Harper Collins, 2011.

Goleman, Daniel, Richard Boyatzis, and Annie McKee. *Primal Leadership: Learning to Lead with Emotional Intelligence.* Boston: Harvard Business School Press, 2002.

Northouse, Peter. *Leadership: Theory and Practice.* Thousand Oaks, CA: Sage, 2005.

Quinn, Robert. *Building the Bridge as You Walk on It.* San Francisco: Jossey-Bass, 2008.

# Our Present Reality

*Toto, I've a feeling we're not in Kansas anymore.*
—Dorothy, in the *Wizard of Oz*

## A Tale of Two Churches

### The Year 1964

The year is 1964. President Lyndon Johnson enacts a number of federal welfare programs, including President Kennedy's original proposal of Medicare, and is re-elected in a landslide over Senator Barry Goldwater. Leonid Brezhnev replaces Nikita Khrushchev as the Soviet leader. Cassius Clay defeats Sonny Liston to win the world heavyweight boxing championship, then changes his name to Muhammad Ali. Popular TV series include *The Man from UNCLE, Outer Limits, Gilligan's Island, Dr. Kildare,* and *The Munsters.* Beatlemania goes global, and adoring fans all over the world make the Beatles' record sales and movie (*A Hard Day's Night*) travel off the charts. According to some sources, not a single juvenile crime is reported in New York City the night of the Beatles' first appearance on *The Ed Sullivan Show* in February 1964.

It is also the heyday of the mainline Christian church. Four years before the great merger of the Methodist Church with the Evangelical

United Brethren Church, new local churches are popping up throughout both denominations. In the Methodist Church, a young associate pastor who performs well during his first four years of ministry is asked to start a new church in what the annual conference believes to be a fast-growing area. There are no detailed demographic studies available, but one can see new housing developments and jobs opening up in this specific community. Without much of a vetting process, the Methodist annual conference bishop and cabinet decide that this associate pastor will be tapped to start a new local congregation. He is given solid support for the year, but there is almost no written literature on starting a church. Even though his district superintendent and bishop are supportive, there are very few specific instructions on how to proceed. The annual conference does help him find a temporary location and promises to provide funding for the purchase of land in the future, if the congregation grows substantially.

This young pastor has been trained primarily in the "programming model" of church ministry in seminary and provided with key youth and educational programs in his first appointment as an associate minister. At his temporary church site, he puts up signs that the church is forming and will start services at this location. A dozen volunteers from nearby churches come out on the weekends to knock on doors and canvass the surrounding neighborhood to inform residents about the new church and invite them to services. The young pastor logs in sixty- to seventy-hour work weeks; soon people drop by and begin to participate in greater numbers. Within the first three years, the church has a membership of seventy-five, and the majority of members are young families with two children. However, adequate funds are not raised, preventing them from reaching self-sufficiency, and their hope to buy their own property and build a church remains out of reach. Although the annual conference is willing to help them put a down payment on a piece of property it does not have the resources to finance a building project. Meanwhile, the pastor's workload is becoming almost unbearable. His family time is suffering greatly, and he has worked himself to the point of burnout. Still, he needs at least twice the membership he currently has in order to be financially viable, and a huge push is necessary in order to grow to that size.

The expectation from his supervisors is that he (and all clergy) work sixty hours or more a week, but he is on the brink of physical exhaustion and quitting the ministry. His district superintendent steps in, allows him to take two months off to recover, and provides pulpit supply for the church.

Needless to say, the church start struggles during the young pastor's ab-

sence. The numbers dwindle to forty active members, and when the pastor returns he is told the annual conference will give him one more year to make a go of it. Renewed by his time off, the pastor is determined to succeed. He also learns some valuable lessons from his first four years. He begins to pace himself better and makes more time for family when he can. He puts his whole self into the next three years, and the church membership doubles. They purchase land with the annual conference's help and over the next three years construct a sanctuary and church school classrooms. The church is helped by the steady stream of visitors and new families who are looking for a church.

After a twelve-year tenure as the founding pastor, he is appointed to a large established church because of his effectiveness in growing this new church start. When he leaves the new church they boast a membership of 275, have a vibrant and active church school and youth groups, and offer many varied programs for almost every age group in the church.

## The Year 2011

Fast forward forty-seven years. In the United States we have seen huge cultural shifts in our society, and they have affected every one of our institutions, especially our religious institutions. We are mired in a huge military conflict that costs more than the country can afford. We have experienced the collapse of our major economic institutions, including the worst stock market crash since the Great Depression, and the nation and world have not recovered financially from these events.

During this time, The United Methodist Church, along with all other mainline denominations, continues on a four-decade slide in membership and attendance and is forced to scale back both financially and programmatically. New churches are being planted not so much out of a missional zeal but because denominational leaders know that, unless they grow and reach out, they have no future.

Against this backdrop, a young associate pastor expresses interest in starting a new church today. The vetting process is completely different from that of the past. This young associate minister must first enroll in a new-church orientation experience and then be tested with a DiSC Profile, to see if she has the ministry gifts to succeed at a new church start. She must undergo a detailed personal interview with a trained assessment professional that looks for clear behavioral indications demonstrating successful leadership abilities resulting in growth. She is under constant assessment to see if her entrepreneurial skills are strong enough to achieve a new church start.

After fairly strong indications that she has the gifts and skill sets to plant a new church, she must go to new-church boot camp for a week, to learn the latest and best techniques and practices for starting a new church.

Next, after extensive training, she undertakes affinity interviews while a specially trained staff person in new-church development tries to match her with the most complementary demographic area. After exhaustive studies, there is a careful match between her own personal affinities (race, age, socioeconomic status, and so forth) and the demographics of the areas available.

She receives from her judicatory a professional coach who has experience planting new churches and now provides coaching for start-up pastors. She would prefer a female coach, but they have few women in this specialized field and none available in her region. The coach works with her on the initial plans for the new church and has regular phone visits to follow up.

A set of detailed benchmarks are established by the pastor and her immediate supervisor, the director of congregational development from the judicatory, her district superintendent, and her coach. The benchmarks also go through a final approval process with the judicatory's oversight committee for all new church starts. The benchmarks are specific and stringent. If she is unable to reach them by the prescribed dates, funding will be pulled from the project and she will have to return to the appointment process for a new assignment. The benchmarks are designed for accountability, but an unintended consequence is the intense pressure they place on church-start pastors.

To avoid the huge expense of providing a full salary *and* start-up costs for a new church plant (called a "parachute drop"), a strong and vital local church (a "mother church"), located in her affinity area, hires her as a half-time associate minister while she does research and sets up for the launch of the new church in a nearby community. A detailed timeline is set up in which by three years she will have accomplished enough in the new area to be able to serve the new church plant full-time.

Volunteer members (from the established mother church where she serves half-time) give one day a week to help her knock on doors and organize the start-up ministry. They collect the names and phone numbers of those who might be interested in the new church, and they organize small-group fellowships around personal interests in order to get people involved. They work extremely hard on this task, but most of the people in this area are not looking for a church home, and many reply that they are just too tired and pressed from their secular jobs to be able to commit their weekends to a church in which they have minimal interest.

The young start-up pastor rents an older movie theater on Sunday mornings to have a temporary space for the church. They put out signs on Sunday morning, but most people are not looking for a church and do not pay attention. After three years of prep work, the church has only twenty-five people involved, and her coach tells her that it is not enough to reach a critical mass for success.

Whereas the new church start of the past, described earlier, was characterized by a neighborhood community that was open to a new church, and even seeking out a church, the present new church start has a dramatically different response. The vast majority of people in the community of the new church start have no interest in affiliating with a church of any denomination or faith. There is not a steady stream of visitors to the church, and for the most part people are oblivious to its presence.

In order to meet new people and recruit for the church, the pastor joins social clubs, gyms, and adult education programs. She attends public gatherings such as book signings, retail grand openings, and civic events. When meeting new people she evangelizes in a new way: not with church tracts and pamphlets (she would be dismissed as a fundamentalist) but with a compelling spiritual invitation. It is the hardest work she has ever done in her ministerial career.

Now in her fourth year, the benchmarks call for her to go three-quarter time at the new church start, having an average attendance of seventy-five people in worship each Sunday, and to be able financially to support one-half of her salary. However, the current average worship attendance at the church is forty-two people, and the new church can pay only one-quarter of the pastor's salary.

Sadly, given the inability of the pastor and new church to reach the designated benchmarks, the judicatory supervisors and committee vote to stop funding and discontinue the new church start. The pastor is given one month to try to provide other church options for those attending, say goodbye, and close the ministry.

# The Difference Between Past and Present, Success and Failure

The differences between these two new church starts are somewhat striking. Notice the lack of assessment, vetting, training, and support systems in the past as compared to the present. Equally noticeable

are the increase of knowledge, organizational refinement, and professional development related to starting a new church in the present as compared to the past.

There are also similarities between these two church starts. They were both pastor-centered, had promising and gifted pastors assigned, and required intense hard work. Both situations put tremendous pressure on the pastors to succeed. Both church plants were in demographically rich and viable communities and received moderate support from the judicatory. And yet, one succeeded while the other failed.

If anything, the more recent church start had much more going for it: a holistic process of assessment, vetting and training of the new church pastor, a more sophisticated and deeper knowledge base of what does and does not work in new church starts, and a competent set of supervisors and learned specialists to coach and mentor the new church pastor.

However, it was not the later church plant that succeeded but the one of the past. Why? One major difference between the two time periods is the great cultural shift that has taken place in regard to organized religion.

In the United States and western Europe, we now live in a society that is post–organized religion. Basically, society has moved from a Christendom era, where the local church is the accepted norm and supported by members of a local community or neighborhood, to a postmodern age that does not value the Christian church and actually shuns organized religion. Statistics point out that 60 percent of the Generation X population has never attended a church, not even for a funeral or wedding.[1] The 2008 Pew Forum on Religion and Public Life reports that approximately one-quarter of American adults (28 percent) have left the faith in which they were raised in favor of another religion, or choose no religion at all.[2]

This same survey reports that the number of people who say they are unaffiliated with any particular faith today is one out of every six Americans (16.1 percent). This figure is more than double the number who say they were not affiliated with any particular religion as children, indicating a growing rejection of organized religious faith. When considering eighteen- to twenty-nine-year-olds who say that they are not affiliated with any particular religion, the number rises to one out of every four Americans.

In the just released religious statistics compiled by the Pew Research Center, these numbers have increased dramatically in just four short years. Presently, one out of every five Americans (19.6%) reports no affiliation with any religious group. In the same young Americans category just men-

tioned, fully one-third of Americans (32%) under the age of thirty have no religious affiliation.[3]

The UMC has not escaped the huge environmental shift in church attendance. The entire denomination lost eighty thousand members in 2004 alone. Today the church loses approximately fifteen thousand members each week.[4]

Between the years 1968 and 2003, the overall population in Los Angeles increased from five million to over fifteen million people. Unfortunately, The United Methodist Church in this region continued to decline in hard numbers. Here are the important statistics:

## Statistics from the California-Pacific Annual Conference

| Year | 1968 | 2003 |
|------|------|------|
| Congregations | 461 | 390 |
| Members | 267,164 | 93,099 |
| Average Worship Attendance | 246 | 41 |
| Ratio of Clergy to Members | 1 to 503 | 1 to 209 |

A more telling description is the fact that Bishop Gerald Kennedy, the icon of membership growth in episcopal leadership, hoped to have one hundred local churches with one thousand members or more by the time he retired. When he did retire in 1972, he had almost reached his goal: ninety-eight churches with one thousand members or more. However, in the thirty-nine years since his retirement, the annual conference has declined in large-membership churches so that they now have only five churches with one thousand members or more.

The sad reality is that these statistics are fairly common for many other United Methodist annual conferences. They are also the norm for many of the mainline Protestant denominations. This is indicative of the United States census statistics that show not one county in the entire nation exists with a greater church population now than it had ten years ago.[5]

A few reasons for this attitudinal shift include: the growing secularity of our world; the increase in competitive alternatives to church in the form

of social media, sports, and retail shopping (think of the dramatic impact retail shopping had on church attendance when stores opened on Sundays); organized religion's own dysfunction, which compels people to leave the faith of their parents; and the failure of organized religion to stay relevant to and inculcate a central purpose in its followers.

There is also the reality of an attitude shift among recent generations toward organized religion. The G.I. generation (born between 1901 and 1924) and the Silent generation (born between 1925 and 1945) comprise what some generational experts label as the "Matures" and make up the backbone of our mainline churches. The Matures believed in institutions, and they gave their time, energy, and money to build them. All of our established and well-endowed institutions, such as hospitals, colleges and universities, public service organizations, and mainline churches, have been maintained and funded by Matures.

The Baby Boomer generation, born between 1948 and 1964, boasts the largest numbers of any of the generations in the United States. Because of the turmoil of the 1960s, Boomers—my generation—grew suspicious of institutions. (I actively protested against the Vietnam War, and my own university as well, because they would not divest some of their endowment in South Africa at the height of the indigenous black struggle against apartheid.) We protested and marched against our institutions because we believed that they were negatively contributing to some of the main ills of our society and world. We envisioned a better future for our world, and we wanted our institutions to change in order to foster that vision.

However, a funny thing happened to the Baby Boomer generation as we grew older and had to make a living: We took jobs and positions of leadership in the very institutions we marched against during our youth. So, we have always had a love-hate relationship with our institutions, but because we became so interwoven with them over time, personally and professionally, our dissidence faded and our loyalty towards them grew.

Along came the postmodern generations (generations X, Y-Millennials, and Z, born between 1968 and the present), who neither love nor hate institutions, but rather find them less relevant to their personal lives. Of course, there are major differences between Gen Xers, Y-Millennials, and Zs. Gen Xers, as the smallest American generation following the largest, the Boomers, have been the most isolated of the modern generations. As such, they have a strong sense of individuality and are more suspicious of

institutions. Boomers acted on their suspicions by protesting to change institutions. In contrast, Gen Xers choose non-affiliation with institutions.

Millennials, on the other hand, have a more positive feeling about institutions, and many experts expect Millennials will develop the same degree of loyalty toward institutions that the Matures demonstrated in the past. The hope is that Millennials will support institutions as a counter to the decline in commitment to institutions as seen in recent years.

One illustration of this comes in the form of giving to institutions. A clergy colleague talks about her Mature-generation parents who give generously to their local church. When they have to miss a Sunday service, they ask one of the children to physically take their weekly pledge commitment to the church. This colleague and her Baby Boomer siblings do not understand why they must hand-deliver their parents' pledge check as opposed to mailing it, or better yet, arranging for an automatic deposit from the bank, which would be most efficient. However, the parents want their pledge to be there on Sunday morning. This is one example of the commitment that the Mature generation has to the church as an institution.

We Baby Boomers can go either way when it comes to giving. Because we have become the institution in so many ways, we feel we must support our institutions financially. However, we have many varied organizations and causes to which we give. Whereas our parents mainly gave their money to one or two institutions, we feel compelled to give to many.

Because of the postmodern generations' indifference toward institutions, they appear less inclined to give to them financially. Although they will give directly to causes that they believe in, causes which make a difference in their community and world, often they don't understand how giving to an institution will help a specific cause.

An example of this is our United Methodist Church program "Imagine No Malaria," which for $10 buys a mosquito net that protects entire families from malaria-infected mosquito bites. Our goal is to eradicate malaria in Sub-Saharan Africa, and many postmoderns will give to a worthy cause such as this. However, they don't always understand how giving to a church provides funds that will go to this particular cause (even though 100 percent of all funds raised for Nothing But Nets goes to purchase and distribute the nets). Because they lack knowledge of the structure of the church, there is little understanding of how giving to it will actually buy nets in Africa.

What this means is that our old system of pledging and apportionments (The United Methodist Church system of supporting the denomina-

tion) will probably not work with younger generations. We will have to find a new way to raise money in the local church and the larger denomination. It is not that younger generations will not give but rather they will find it difficult to support an institution like our mainline denominations without a cause worthy of their commitments.

The actual generational giving statistics support these assumptions. Taken from the Campbell and Company's generational giving analysis we find:

- **Matures:** 77 percent gave toward religious purposes, and the average that persons of faith gave to religious institutions In 2006 was $1,209.60. 57.7 percent attend church once a week.

- **Boomers:** 46.7 percent gave toward religious purposes, and the average that persons of faith gave to religious institutions in 2006 was $1,380.90. 32.5 percent attend church once a week.

- **Generation X:** 45.1 percent gave toward religious purposes, and the average that persons of faith gave to religious institutions in 2006 was $1,362.60. 30.8 percent attend church once a week.

- **Millennials:** 41.5 percent gave toward religious purposes, and the average that persons of faith gave to religious institutions in 2006 was $722.10. 27.9 percent attend church once a week.[6]

From these statistics it is surprising to see that Boomers and Gen Xers are very close in what they give to religious causes in per capita dollars. However, what also stands out is the huge drop in regular church attendance by all later generations as compared with Matures. As Indiana University's Center on Philanthropy has concluded, the prime indicator of giving to the church is weekly church attendance, and future giving patterns will likely decrease with less commitment to attend church.[7]

# A Post–Organized Religion Culture

In summary, we in the Western hemisphere live in a culture that is now post–organized religion. In the past, it was a given that one would attend a

local church. Now there is no such expectation, and the secular population does not value church affiliation. This cultural shift has thrown the mainline Christian church for a loop. The old church systems were designed to work for the previous cultural milieu: an "attractional" model where people came to church. What is now called for is a "reset" of our entire Christian ministry, and such a reset starts with our leadership.

# For Further Reading: The Postmodern Church

Butler-Bass, Diana. *Christianity after Religion: The End of Church and the Birth of a New Spiritual Awakening*. New York: HarperCollins, 2012.

Clayton, Philip. *Transforming Christian Theology: For Church and Society*. Minneapolis: Fortress Press, 2009.

Creasy Dean, Kenda. *Almost Christian: What the Faith of Our Teenagers Is Telling the American Church*. New York: Oxford UP, 2010.

Hirsch, Alan. *The Forgotten Ways: Reactivating the Missional Church*. Grand Rapids: Brazos Press, 2006.

Hirsch, Alan, and Michael Frost. *The Shaping of Things to Come: Innovation and Mission for the 21ˢᵗ Century Church*. Grand Rapids: Baker Books, 2003.

McLaren, Brian. *A New Kind of Christianity: Ten Questions That Are Transforming the Faith*. New York: HarperCollins, 2010.

Putnam, Robert, and David E. Campbell. *American Grace: How Religion Divides and Unites Us*. New York: Simon and Schuster, 2010.

Tickle, Phyllis. *The Great Emergence: How Christianity Is Changing and Why*. Grand Rapids: Baker Books, 2008.

Weems, Lovett. *Focus: The Real Challenges That Face the United Methodist Church*. Nashville: The United Methodist Publishing House, 2011.

CHAPTER 3

# The Big Three of Spiritual Leadership

*If you go to Aikido studio just to learn the physical techniques, that is
like breaking into a bank and stealing the furniture.*
—Gaku Homma, sensei (teacher)

The premise of this book is that spiritual leadership is not ingrained
but rather can be improved. In order to provide a grounding of this premise, let us take a look at one conceptual model that church consultant Gil
Rendle often uses: "Inputs—Throughputs—Outputs."

One can think of inputs as all of the raw materials that we as individuals start with: our intelligence, relational ability, resilience, attitudes, and
so on. Our outputs are our ideals of a true leader: a mentor who serves as
a model and has qualities such as courage, wisdom, and compassion, or
simply has the attributes of the top performers in our field. In the case of
spiritual leaders, all of these factors come into play. There are role models
in ministry to whom we look up to and seek to emulate. There are traits
and qualities in these role models that we admire: deep faith roots, preaching ability, social skills, charisma, and so on. We can also think of the top
spiritual leaders that we know, and one can objectively isolate the attributes
that such high-performing clergy have in common.

Finally, the throughputs are those systems, growth opportunities, and

learning experiences that shape and mold us into leadership. A leadership development system, or lack thereof, is an example of a throughput. However, throughputs can also include almost any learning experience or growth opportunity. Reading a book, taking a class, or going through a training workshop are all examples of throughputs toward the objective of better leadership. If one desires to become a better spiritual leader, all three of these elements must be present.

# Inputs

One might think that there is nothing you can do about inputs, or the present condition. After all, it is somewhat a question of nature and experience. However, it is critical in this first stage to want or desire to become a better spiritual leader. One's beginning attitude is absolutely critical. If one has no motivation to become a better leader, then no amount of throughputs, or development and training experiences, will have much effect.

We in United Methodist cabinets (bishops and district superintendents who appoint clergy to local churches) often speak of a pastor's "teachability." If for whatever reason a pastor is not teachable, there is little hope for improvement, and such clergy are usually very low in effectiveness. So teachability and motivation to improve are key elements in the input phase of leadership development.

My definition of teachability has to do with the ability to integrate what one learns into one's daily craft. Most of us learn all kinds of things, but how many of us integrate our learning into our behaviors and actions? Intellectual learning has no effect on life unless it is applied toward some relevant action or behavior. The so-called halo effect, whereby a person exhibits temporary changes in behavior after intensive training but eventually returns to the same default behaviors, is an example of failing to integrate new learning. There are many reasons why someone might not be teachable: on a continuum, from thinking that they know everything (egocentricity) to being unable to appropriate what they have learned. However, the foundation of teachability is putting into action or behavior what one learns.

Closely related to this concept is the quality of lifelong learning. The top-performing clergy have a hunger and desire to learn and grow throughout their entire career. Although many of the top-performing clergy in any denomination have reached a stage of "mastery" of the art of ministry, they are never satisfied with their knowledge or skill level. In fact, if one thinks

she has mastered it all, that is usually an indicator that she is not one of the top performers among her peers.

One of the key abilities here is how much information, experience, or skill one can absorb. For example, it is often observed of child prodigies that they have the ability to appropriate or absorb huge amounts of data or input. The average person retains 10 to 15 percent of new learning, but if one can increase the amount that is being absorbed, one's development will also increase exponentially.

The perfect example of this is the reading of a very conceptually dense textbook. One can read for hours on end and eventually complete the book, but if one doesn't retain any of the ideas, that person will not have learned anything from the reading experience. One of the keys to leadership development is increasing our capacity to absorb greater quantities of data and appropriate it. There are specific techniques to accomplish this, but it starts with a person's motivation to learn and develop.

# Outputs

Of equal importance is the output, or end product of the leadership development process. The key question to ask is, What type of spiritual leader do you want to be? The adjectives commonly used in response to this question are also important: "the best, the top performer, the most effective." All of these adjectives lack precision and behavioral actions. Our fuzziness about what the final output is derails our chance of improvement. We have to have a clear conception of what we want to improve at and what our ideal of leadership truly is.

In an organizational sense, this continues to plague the ordination and development of clergy. If a board of ordained ministry, or a judicatory equivalent of the vetting and credentialing of its clergy, does not have a clear conception of what the final output is, how can it achieve its objective? As our mainline denominations continue to shrink in members and local churches, there is great pressure to bring in those spiritual leaders who will make a difference in their ministry. Without a clear description of what type of spiritual leader a denomination needs, the output will continue to be disappointing.

The "how to" takeaway in becoming a better spiritual leader here is to have the end in mind: what is your ideal in a spiritual leader? What role models in ministry do you aspire to be like? If you want to become a great spiritual leader, what would that look like?

Personally, I think the best spiritual leaders practice their faith. In this sense, faith becomes a verb, as one "faiths" by putting the inner spirit into practice. The most mature spiritual leaders that I have encountered demonstrate that their inner belief structure is consistent with their outer actions. They possess a deep well of faith, and it is displayed in their actions and behaviors. Interestingly enough, this is the same consistency involved in integrity: that one's inner character is consistent with one's outer behavior.

Another major piece on the output side is to determine which gaps in my present leadership need to be filled. What do I need to work on? What leadership skill sets do I need to improve and hone? This personal assessment piece is a very difficult thing to do alone. As human beings we have the tendency to fool ourselves on a rather constant basis, often thinking we have performed better than we really have. In order to get a more objective understanding of our personal leadership, we need the observations of those around us. Currently, the best tool available for this is a well-crafted "360-degree assessment." Typically, a good 360-degree assessment will include our supervisors, peers, those we supervise, and those who relate to our ministry both near and far away.

I recently took a highly professional 360-degree assessment that ranked me with other secular executives and leaders. All of my major leadership traits and characteristics were scored in comparison with their database of other leaders. The results of this particular 360-degree assessment were visualized in a circle, and leadership strengths were balanced on the other side of the circle with possible weaknesses. I found this data very helpful, as there is usually a "shadow side" to qualities and traits. Good leaders see this continuum and make allowances for their shadow side tendencies.

However, the real payoff was in the personal comments that people made about my leadership. Here, there was a cluster of comments that referenced my tendency to be impatient, especially with the pace of change in the church. The implication was that it affected my leadership in a negative way.

This 360-degree assessment called for a debriefing with the person who administered it as well as other coaches one might be working with. I discussed the results with two people, and having the chance to talk through the issues with an objective third party was extremely helpful.

For example, I believed that I press hard for change because of the urgency of our present situation. In other words, it was not impatience on my part but urgency. My coach was able to point out that this may be the

reason why I am behaving in a certain way, but those around me are seeing it as impatience, not urgency. That was clearly documented in the comments. In order to improve on this behavior, I have to first acknowledge it as a problem and then come up with ways that I will address it in my actual future behavior. For me, I addressed it in my individual development plan (IDP). What follows is an example of this component of my IDP.

### Goals to Address Personal Challenges:

1. Work on perceived "impatience"

WHY: From my latest 360 evaluation, a few comments centered on my perceived impatience.

HOW: Work on behavior change

FROM (Source, e.g., 360, SPRC Eval., etc.): 360 Evaluation

### Specific Objectives (in detail)

A. Reflect with my executive coach on this issue.

B. Explain my concern for urgency when perceived impatience arises.

C. Temper my emotional level when it comes to the issues of urgency.

D. Reflect on the critical distinction between urgency and impatience.

E. Monitor this behavior with the cabinet (the district superintendents with whom I work most closely).

### Start Date: Immediate

As one can see from this IDP example, the focus is on my behavior. In order to become a better leader, I am attempting to change a behavior that may hinder that leadership. I hope it is also clear that I probably would not have identified this problem on my own. Even the best leaders are very poor judges of their own behavior. I needed an objective external source to make me aware of the problem, and in this case, the 360-degree assessment fulfilled that purpose.

In many ways the 360-degree assessment and individual development plan can be seen as the tools of the throughputs, or that which shapes us to become better leaders. Once we have the motivation to improve and grow as a spiritual leader, and once we have an idea of what kind of leader we want to be and what we need to work on to get there, the systems, techniques, and tools of leadership help us to achieve that goal.

The myriad of workshops, training events, and development processes available to us are too numerous to mention. One could study and learn by oneself or enroll in a course or program. One could learn from a trusted mentor, coach, or peer group. The opportunities for growth and learning are endless, and most denominations are offering their own specific training and development programs for their clergy.

It should become clear that on the front end of inputs, one needs to have the commitment to grow and change to become a better leader. On the opposite end, the outputs require one to know what the leadership objectives are. The specific question to ask is what kind of strong spiritual leader one wants to be. Also, what leadership skill sets and qualities does one need in order to become that leader?

I believe strongly in the need of clergy to reinvent themselves throughout their career. As I have moved through the typical size dimensions of local churches in my own pastoral career, I have noticed the need to grow into the type of leader that the next size ministry calls for. In other words, if you start at a family-size church (fifty or fewer average worship service attendance) and their need at this size is for the minister to serve as a chaplain, then in order to grow, one needs to act with the mindset of the next larger size church, or pastoral size (up to 150 average worship service attendance). The role identification of the pastoral-size church is for the minister to be shepherd, and this requires that much of the ministry surround the pastor. Whereas the laity call the shots for the family-size church, clearly the clergy call the shots for the pastoral-size setting. Many local churches plateau at 150 in worship, but that is primarily because the minister refuses to give up power to the laity and becomes the main bottleneck for the church to grow larger. Research has shown that human beings have an absolute limit on their ability to stay in personal relationship with a number exceeding 150 people, and that is exactly what is going on when a church reaches this level. The pastor cannot manage a larger number than 150, and growth beyond that point is stymied by the pastor.

One way to break out of the pastoral-size plateau is for the pastor to change role identifications again and become a resource leader, empowering laity and groups to take both responsibility and authority for ministry directly. This will usher in the next size transition, or program-size church (up to 350 average worship attendance). Notice the difficulty in the transition from pastoral to program: the pastor is rewarded and applauded for being the center of ministry in the pastoral size and yet must give up that whole identification in moving to the program size. This is the reason that so

many clergy get tripped up when they take on a program-size church for the first time in their career, or why they never are able to move their pastoral-size church to the program level. All that they know and have had success at has been to be the center of ministry in the pastoral size; now they must give that up in order to lead the program-size church. It takes a tremendous amount of behavioral change in order to make this particular transition.

Beyond that, one enters into the corporate-size church, and the pastor must morph again in role identification. In large corporate churches the pastor must take on figurehead-leader status, manage a large staff that carries out the ministry, and provide the vision, alignment, and direction of the church in more of a CEO-type model.

Of course, this is a simplified summary of the complexity of size transitions of churches. The point is that at each growth interval, ministers must reinvent themselves into different types of pastoral leaders. One usually finds that those highly successful clergy who have grown their churches throughout their career have stayed at the church for a very long time and have been able to reinvent themselves in ministry as the church has grown. One will also find that the megachurch pastors who have built churches to that level have a whole host of other leadership gifts, but had they not been willing to engage in lifelong growth and reinvention, they would not have had the success that they have had. All of us can engage in this practice of lifelong learning and development and so reinvent ourselves to a higher level of leadership.

# Do This, Not That!

The key prescriptive behavior here is a deep curiosity coupled with a hunger to learn on a sustained basis. It starts with our awareness that we are all novices, and life itself involves constant learning that leads to growth. One never arrives at a final apex of truth and mastery; rather, the joy is in the journey of constant new learning. If our plate is too full or too empty, we are not on this learning journey. What we should not do is to think we have the right answers for any form of ministry and force those answers onto others and the church. In adaptive leadership there are no road maps available, and success in the past does not necessarily mean success for the present and future due to the constantly changing contexts of our society and world. The most successful among us will be constantly adapting to new surroundings and contexts, and this means flexibility and learning as primary behaviors. As in Goleman's concept of using styles of leadership for

the specific situation, we need to adapt our ministry style to the next level of church size we would like the church to grow into.

I want to add a quick word to those spiritual leaders who believe they know it all in ministry and no longer need any new information: you will not grow in your spiritual leadership. It is often a very subtle arrogance when a pastor dismisses certain information as irrelevant, or indicates that he or she knows about this or that already. Not only does it display a lack of teachability but the arrogance is clearly noticeable and does not sit well with colleagues or supervisors.

As mentioned before, we are in a time of ministry where no one knows the answers, and our entire approach must be constant learning and experimentation to discover what might work in our own context. The thought has often crossed my mind that it is presumptuous to write a book on leadership when I know so little and have so few answers to the pressing questions asked by our mainline denominations. So we find ourselves in a time of spiritual kaizen, where all of us need to learn on a continual basis, grow stronger in our spirituality and leadership daily, and trust that God will provide the means to lead our churches out of the present wilderness.

# Throughputs

A quick word about throughputs in the context of the systems of the church: it has been well documented that the present systems an organization has in place produce the results for which that system has been designed. Since many denominations are unclear about the type of pastor they need for the adaptive challenges of the future, their present system continues to produce the same type of pastor as in the past. Hence, seminaries, or the educational systems for clergy in training, evaluative boards, and vetting agencies of the denomination tend to produce that which the group or organization sees as the ideal output. A case in point would be our United Methodist Church system that requires a basic ordination degree (Master of Divinity) in order to pursue ordination as an elder in the church. Currently the UMC has thirteen denominational seminaries geographically spread across the United States. In addition to this, we allow our seminary candidates to go to non–United Methodist seminaries that have been approved by our University Senate and accreditation bodies. Since all of these seminaries have their own incorporation status and standing, the church does not have control over the curriculum or content of what is being taught. Of course, I support higher education's right to

academic freedom, and I do not believe the church should prescribe to the seminary what to teach. However, the church and academy should be in close partnership, especially regarding inputs, throughputs, and outputs.

Since the seminary is providing much of the throughputs for the church in terms of training and development, a mutually agreed upon output of the ideal minister should be discussed and worked on. In the crude sense of the church being the customer of what the seminary is producing, the seminary must stay in close communication with the church about what is needed. Currently, many of our churches are in turnaround situations, and a large percentage of them are on the edge of demise. Preparing ministerial candidates for the realities of what they will be facing upon graduation is absolutely critical at this time. Right now, some of the skill sets I see as absolutely critical for the ministry are adaptive leadership, resiliency, entrepreneurism, discipleship systems, networking, and mission field engagement. We will talk more about these qualities and skill sets later in the book.

I cannot emphasize enough the crucial time that the church and academy find themselves in and the essential need to be working together. We have to address the reset of our ministry agenda as we both face the prospects of diminishing numbers and resources.

The vast majority of mainline clergy are educated in our seminary system, which despite denominational differences, has remarkable similarities and consistencies. The majority of our mainline seminaries have a faculty that is trained in their disciplines by the university model of critical scholarship. The majority of our seminary faculty members receive honors and accolades not from their church affiliation but through their own academic disciplinary guilds and their publishing records. There is nothing inherently wrong with this system; it is simply the reality of our academic world.

However, our present church-seminary system does not facilitate the best relationship between the church and the academy. Communication does not always flow directly between the two, and more often than not, there is criticism on both sides of the fence. Mainly, the church is concerned about the product of the seminary—the candidates the seminary educates—and is critical of the candidates' lack of preparation for the new challenges the church faces. On the other hand, the seminary is critical of the church in not understanding the ethos of academic freedom, and the fact that they produce a well-rounded and academically grounded candidate. Having served on both sides, I see the tensions more clearly, and in defense of both institutions, I think the academy must work more directly with the needs of the church and that the church must reduce its huge expectations of the seminary.

Toward this end, the church must pay more attention to the seminary in the form of communication and financial support. The church must do better in making their case for what they need in the skill sets and training of candidates. Many faculty members simply do not understand the present context of the church's decline and the fact that many candidates will be sent to local churches that are on the edge of demise.

Many of our current seminaries are also fighting for their own financial survival, and the church must increase support and revenue, not diminish it. Since both institutions are faced with a new world of change, long-term planning, pruning, and direction should be performed as a joint venture instead of one institution existing in isolation from the other.

The church must also lessen its expectation of what the seminary can and cannot do. A three-year Master of Divinity program can provide the basic foundation of the academic disciplines but cannot provide all of the necessary skill sets that are currently needed in facing our adaptive challenges. The church and seminary need to work together to forge a comprehensive residency program in which they truly complement each other. The seminary should not be expected to provide best practices in stewardship, adaptive leadership, evangelism and outreach, and all the other areas that the church is crying out for. These are areas that the church itself must augment in the candidate's residency period. When I was a young faculty member of one of our seminaries, my theological mentor John Cobb would often say that his understanding of what the seminary is to provide its students is to "be critical reflectors on the church and world."[1] I agree with John on this point, and unless the church wants to pay for a five-year degree, it is unwise to expect the seminary to provide the practical tools of ministry for its candidates.

Likewise, the seminary must be more open to the end product it produces: a postmodern clergy candidate who is grounded in the traditional disciplines but who has an open mindset about the church and world. Adaptation in ministry is going to be a fundamental necessity, and those candidates who have a rigid and fixed mental model of what the church should be will not fare well.

Stanford University psychologist Carol Dweck has done extensive research on the nature of mindsets, or our beliefs about ourselves and our own qualities. She posits two opposite mindsets: first, a fixed mindset that believes one's basic qualities—like intelligence and talent—are genetic traits that we either possess or do not possess. Typically the fixed mindset comes

with the attitude that we can do nothing to enhance such qualities and that they are the sole determining factor of our success or failure. With this mindset usually comes the belief that we do not have to work hard at developing our God-given qualities, rather they are simply there by genetic good fortune.

Dweck calls the second mindset a growth mindset, in which one believes that our most basic qualities can be developed and grown through hard work and practice. Yes, we are endowed with a basic core genetic foundation of intelligence and abilities, but what we do with these abilities makes all the difference. We can either squander them away through disuse, or we can continually hone and practice our abilities to reach higher levels of accomplishment. With this growth mindset usually comes the commitment to continually work on our abilities, and the outcome is both lifelong learning and a resilience that builds on defeats and setbacks in a positive way. Highly effective clergy usually possess a growth mindset, and it manifests itself in their life practices: lifelong learning and resiliency to bounce back from defeats and setbacks.

In addition to the basic knowledge grounding in the academic disciplines of seminary (biblical studies, theology, ethics, church history, preaching, pastoral counseling, education, administration, and so forth), forging the growth mindset is fundamental for both the church and seminary. The church and seminary must work together to forge an ethos of the growth mindset.

Finally, the church must also take a hard look at its traditional throughputs in leadership development. Are our local churches and judicatories producing the type of leaders our church needs for the present challenges and future? Are our Christian education programs producing children and adults who will be strong and loyal church members? Are our discipling systems producing transformed disciples who are committed to transform their communities and world? These are key questions that every local church, judicatory, and denomination needs to ask and take a hard look at.

Systems fragmentation is also a major concern for most judicatories. For example, is there coordination and a smooth handoff between campus ministry and short-term missionary programs and the local church? What about between campus ministry and young adult programs in the local church? In many instances, each of these systems operates in isolation from the other, and we must find a way to develop a coordinated and aligned leader-development process that provides a smooth handoff from one system to the next.

# The First of the Big Three: A Deep Well of Faith

We can provide a steady stream of appetizers on leadership development before the main course, but we now need to get to the meat and potatoes of our purpose: improving our spiritual leadership. I believe there are three major foundations that all spiritual leaders need to possess: a deep well of faith, emotional intelligence, and transformational leadership.

In my research with highly effective clergy, all of them regularly referenced their own faith as the main resource of their pastoral leadership. These highly effective pastors possess a deep and grounding faith that does impact their leadership in a number of interlocking ways. Their faith starts with forming the core identity of who they are and why they are in ministry in the first place. It is the central part of their own core values, and provides the necessary grounding for their ministry. Their faith also provides the grounding for some other key themes: vision, humility, resilience, and passion in ministry.

The biblical story of Jesus' encounter with the Samaritan woman at the well we referenced earlier is a good bridge to the deep faith possessed by highly effective clergy, and a constant reminder of the need for faith in spiritual leadership. "The water of eternal life, where one will thirst no more" is the lifeblood of our ministry that sustains us, and also the substance of what we offer to others.

This water that God in Christ offers is like the fuel of our ministry. Without it we will become depleted and exhausted, as the crush of people's needs are always greater than our own capacity to meet such needs. Unless we continually drink from the well of eternal life, we will be over-stressed and burn out rather quickly.

In addressing liberation theology's spirituality, parent of all liberation theology Gustavo Gutiérrez wrote the book *We Drink from Our Own Wells*, adapting the title from the words of St. Bernard of Clairvaux, who said, "Everyone has to drink from his own well." In a beautiful description of the Christian faith Gutiérrez writes,

> A Christian is defined as a follower of Jesus, and reflection
> on the experience of following constitutes the central theme
> of any solid theology. The experience and the reflection alike
> have for their subject a community that under the movement

of the Spirit focuses its life on the proclamation of the good news: the Lord is risen! Death and injustice are not the final word of history. Christianity is a message of life, a message based on the gratuitous love of the Father for us.[2]

Gutiérrez believes that our Christian message of life springs from the deep well of faith, and the whole community of believers can drink from such life-giving waters. In fact, if clergy neglect their spiritual life, they will be cut off from the very source of life itself, and be unable to carry out ministry with integrity and depth.

So, the very foundation of spiritual leadership begins with the deep well of faith, and clergy must continue to practice spiritual disciplines and grow stronger in their own faith journey throughout their entire careers.

One might think of faith as one of the primary foundations of ministry that no clergy can do without, and yet, it cannot be the only foundation for effective ministry. To use a sports analogy, a baseball player needs the fundamental of being able to throw a baseball, and even pitchers have to combine other fundamentals like fielding and base-running to excel in the sport.

Likewise, all clergy need faith as a fundamental foundation, but ministry calls for other fundamentals and skill sets in order to succeed. For example, I have seen some clergy almost exclusively focus on spirituality and spiritual disciplines in their ministry, but be unable to lead a congregation to growth and vitality.

In my research on highly effective clergy leadership, lifelong growth in both spiritual depth and leadership skills is necessary to achieve greatness in the ministry.

## Do This, Not That!

My prescriptive advice here is that spiritual depth and growth forms the foundation of our well of living water, and we must give primary attention to our spiritual development. However, the demands of modern ministry mean that we must have other tools and skill sets to lead the church, and we cannot focus on spiritual development alone. Adaptive spiritual leadership means that we must learn and grow in entrepreneurial and innovative ministry, change and transformational models, and systems theory, to name just a few. However, to focus solely on leadership skills and learning will leave us dry and burned out. Both spirituality and leadership growth are necessary to meet the demands of the twenty-first-century church.

# The Second of the Big Three: Emotional Intelligence

This provides a good segue to another foundation for spiritual leadership: emotional intelligence. Emotional intelligence, or EQ, is a relatively new concept, but it has vast implications in effective leadership. EQ researchers John Mayer, Peter Salovey, and David Caruso define emotional intelligence as "the ability to perceive and express emotion, assimilate emotion in thought, understand and reason with emotion, and regulate emotion in the self and others."[3] The foundation of emotional intelligence is in the building of formal and informal relationships.

There are four areas of emotional intelligence: the first is self-recognition, which is composed of emotional self-awareness, accurate self-assessment, and self-confidence. The second area is self-regulation, which is made up of six attributes: emotional self-control, trustworthiness, conscientiousness, adaptability, achievement drive, and initiative. The third is other-recognition, which includes three characteristics: empathy, service, and organizational awareness. The last is other-regulation, which builds relationships through developing others, influence, communication, conflict management, catalyzing change, visionary leadership, building bonds, and teamwork and collaboration.

Researchers Daniel Goleman, Richard Boyatzis, and Annie McKee provide the most popular breakdown of the EQ categories:

***Personal Competence: These capabilities determine how we manage ourselves.***

### Self-Awareness

Emotional self-awareness: Reading one's own emotions and recognizing their impact, using "gut sense" to guide decisions.

Accurate self-assessment: Knowing one's strengths and limits.

Self-confidence: A sound sense of one's self-worth and capabilities.

### Self-Management

Emotional self-control: Keeping disruptive emotions and impulses under control.

Transparency: Displaying honesty and integrity, trustworthiness.

Adaptability: Flexibility in adapting to changing situations or overcoming obstacles.

Achievement: The drive to improve performance to meet inner standards of excellence.

Initiative: Readiness to act and seize opportunities.

Optimism: Seeing the upside in events.

**Social Competence: These capabilities determine how we manage relationships.**

*Social Awareness*

Empathy: Sensing others' emotions, understanding their perspective, and taking active interest in their concerns.

Organizational awareness: Reading the currents, decision networks, and politics at the organizational level.

Service: Recognizing and meeting follower, client, or customer needs.

*Relationship Management*

Inspirational leadership: Guiding and motivating with a compelling vision.

Influence: Wielding a range of tactics for persuasion.

Developing others: Bolstering others' abilities through feedback and guidance.

Change catalyst: Initiating, managing, and leading in a new direction.

Conflict management: Resolving disagreements.

Building bonds: Cultivating and maintaining a web of relationships.

Teamwork and collaboration: Fostering cooperation and team building.[4]

In my research, I was able to establish a quantitative correlation at the .05 level that showed that highly effective UMC clergy excelled in emotional intelligence as compared to less effective clergy. Such results are scientifically conclusive: highly effective clergy demonstrate high EQ.

# Self-Awareness

## *Emotional Self-Awareness and Knowing One's Strengths and Limits*

In the first category of personal competence, highly effective spiritual leaders demonstrate high self-awareness. They are keenly aware of their impact on others around them, and use this sense as an intuitive guide to both extend and temper their influence over others. They know when to push forward and pull back when it comes to working with people. Self-awareness also includes knowing one's strengths and weaknesses, and in leadership this is critical to know what one can and cannot do in ministry.

For example, highly effective ministers leverage their strengths by leading in areas where they are personally competent and find other individuals to assist in the areas where they are weaker or less passionate. They are motivated enough to work on their areas of weakness, but once they reach a level of basic competence they find others who excel in such areas and empower them to do that work.

Personally and professionally, my role is to work at both the thirty-thousand-foot level and on the ground. As the "spiritual and temporal leader of an annual conference," I am tasked to see the big picture and work strategically to align the annual conference toward its purpose and mission. This task also engages my own personal strengths: strategic, vision driven, and conceptual thinking. My Gallup StrengthsFinder signature strengths are: Strategic, Futuristic, Achiever, Relational, and Competitive. I have had to work at tasks that include details and comprehensive planning that involves minutiae, but clearly it is not something I enjoy. To compensate I make sure I am surrounded by detail-oriented staff and personnel. Both my administrative assistant and assistant to the bishop excel with tracking details and keep me from going crazy when I forget the time and location of an offsite appointment. The point here is to manage one's weaknesses by acknowledging them and then working with others who excel at the things you are not strong at or have less interest in.

## *Self-Confidence*

Knowing oneself well also enhances self-confidence. Starting with one's strengths and acknowledging one's weaknesses is a freeing exercise, and it mitigates having to hide weaknesses for fear of being judged. In the martial arts there is an old adage that says if you do not know yourself or your op-

ponent, then the odds of your success are very low. If you know yourself and not your opponent, or the reverse, the odds go up to 50 percent success. However, if you know both yourself and your opponent, you have maximized your possibility of success, and you need not fear any conflict.

And yet, we all know how contextual self-confidence is. Often the most gifted individuals struggle with self-doubt. I have encountered many young clergy who have so many more gifts than I do, and yet, in their self-disclosing moments they express the fear of failing, or of not succeeding. So, a past history of success is important to draw from, but you will probably find a lot of failures sprinkled into that mix.

Two important qualities are connected to self-confidence: a risk-taking perspective rather than a risk-averse perspective and a healthy resilience. In this regard, all of the highly effective pastors I studied had the courage to take risks, and were not too concerned about the systemic consequences of failing. One pastor said, "Don't bet the farm, but short of that, be willing to take measured risks for the sake of what will be learned in the process."

For judicatory leaders and supervisors, there is a clear lesson here: we must create a culture that rewards healthy risk-taking and does not punish when taking a risk does not pay off. As a bishop, I am always encouraging pastors to be risk taking, not risk averse, and although the affirmation is helpful, unless the system can truly back up your words, clergy will continue to take the safe route. So, it is the culture itself that must reinforce risk-taking, and any semblance of being punished if a risk does not pan out will harm such a cultural value. Lately, I have been thinking that churches need to have at least one of what Jim Collins calls BHAGs ("Big Hairy Audacious Goals"). I would like to include one other letter in the form of "S" to represent the word "scary." "BSHAG" would stand for "Big, Scary, Hairy, Audacious Goal." Here, unless we are truly scared or fearful, the goal probably doesn't have enough risk involved in it. Again, we shouldn't bet the farm, but we should be willing to have enough risk involved that it would make a true difference if we succeed.

In my own research I have been trying to adapt the secular business models around risk management to apply to the church. Some of these models are quite complicated and not easily explained to faith-based leaders. However, Jim Collins recently articulated one of the best analogies that I have ever heard on risk management. In their book *Great by Choice*, Collins and Morton Hansen advocate the principle "fire bullets, then cannonballs":[5]

Picture yourself at sea, a hostile ship bearing down on you. You have a limited amount of gunpowder. You take all your gunpowder and use it to fire a big cannonball. The cannonball flies out over the ocean . . . and misses the target, off by 40 degrees. You turn to your stockpile and discover you're out of gunpowder. You die.

But suppose instead that when you see the ship bearing down, you take a little bit of gunpowder and fire a bullet. It misses by 40 degrees. You make another bullet and fire. It misses by 30 degrees. You make a third bullet and fire, missing only by 10 degrees. The next bullet hits—ping!—the hull of the oncoming ship. Now, you take all the remaining gunpowder and fire a big cannonball along the same line of sight, which sinks the enemy ship. You live.[6]

Collins and Hansen see 10X companies (those that not only survive but thrive during periods of great turmoil and downturns) as consistently managing risk by firing bullets before cannonballs. They see bullets as low-cost, low-risk, and low-distraction for the organization, and they track the potential of finding the target that would mean greater success in the near future.

Once the bullet finds the correct target or strategy, a calibrated cannonball is fired where significant resources and energy can be put to achieve the goal. For Collins and Hansen, calibrated cannonballs are based in "empirical validation," or the facts and data that make the risk of a cannonball worth the firing.[7]

This is opposed to uncalibrated cannonballs that have no actual basis in fact or experience and create havoc when they do not hit anything close to success. The organization spends enormous time, expense, and energy for a wild shot in the dark. It may seem courageous at the time, but if it doesn't produce results, it is quickly labeled foolhardy, and sometimes leads to the demise of the organization.

A perfect example of an uncalibrated cannonball is a new church start that launches a regular worship service too quickly. Let's say a new church pastor has a constituency list of two hundred, and their preview worship services have averaged fifty people. The funding demands and time constraints are pressing in on the new church start, and without some key systems developed (communications, welcoming, leadership, and discipling)

the new start pastor decides to launch regular worship services. The prevailing wisdom is that one needs double the numbers of constituents and preview worship attendees before a successful launch, and instead of firing more bullets to hone his or her aim, the pastor fires an uncalibrated cannonball in one huge opening launch. Seventy-five people show up at that first Sunday, but then the numbers dwindle each successive week, so after a month the new church start is only averaging forty-five in worship, and they never recover from the uncalibrated cannonball.

On the other hand, take the example of a turnaround church in a changing demographic neighborhood. The original Anglo congregation is aging and small, and the neighborhood has changed to mostly second generation Mexican American. The pastor, who is bilingual in Spanish and English, starts firing bullets in the form of small interest groups for the Latino neighbors: potty training classes for parents with infant children, after school tutoring days for neighborhood kids, financial management classes for young families. She calibrates what seems to attract the church's neighbors and what doesn't. She keeps experimenting with different programs, and realizes that the data focuses around the need for a first-rate children's ministry. She projects a calibrated cannonball in the form of a vacation Bible school program that will launch a series of ongoing programs for the neighborhood children and families. The church goes all out to fire the cannonball in the summer, and it is a smashing success with over three hundred children in attendance. With the flywheel turning, she then launches her children's ministry that will attract young families. The church begins to rejuvenate, and after firing bullets on a new worship design, neighborhood families start coming on Sunday. The worship service doubles in attendance and the church is well on the way to a successful turnaround.

Collins and Hansen outline their overall strategy for "firing bullets, then cannonballs":

- Fire bullets.

- Assess: Did your bullets hit anything?

- Consider: Do any of your successful bullets merit conversion to a big cannonball?

- Convert: Concentrate resources and fire a cannonball once calibrated.

• Don't fire uncalibrated cannonballs.

• Terminate bullets that show no evidence of eventual success.[8]

In my estimation, this is one of the clearest articulations of risk management and experimentation that I have seen. If our clergy and churches can follow these principles (and they absolutely need to experiment in this way), local churches will have the best shot at becoming or remaining vital.

Coupled with risk-taking is the quality of resilience. Again, all of the highly effective pastors demonstrated resiliency in their lives and ministerial careers. All of them had experienced personal and professional setbacks, but their way of dealing with such problems was to turn to their faith. Often mentioned were faith, prayer, and spiritual disciplines that enabled them to bounce back from a setback. It reinforced the deep well of faith necessary in order to thrive in ministry.

The other deep take-away from interviews with highly effective clergy was what they learned and how they grew after a setback. Many of them mentioned the important learning and self-awareness that came from failure or a life transition. One pastor put his learning into the context of facing burnout in trying to change a church where he was appointed. His spiritual director taught him the metaphor of trying to cut through the bone of fresh poultry that he was preparing to cook. If you try to chop through the bone itself, you will encounter great difficulty, so you need to look for the joints, the spaces between the bones, to cut through. In applying this concept to his ministry, this pastor commented that he grew weary trying to force change. He describes an alternative method: "Maybe my way of being resilient has been to be able to step back and find the space and then move into it in a different way."[9]

## Self-Management

### Emotional Self-Control

In terms of the second major area of self-management, we can recall instances when clergy trip themselves up by failing to control themselves. Here, emotional self-control is essential for success in the people-oriented profession of ministry. So much of the ministry involves intra-personal communication, and knowing the appropriate response is absolutely critical. We need to be authentic in ministry, but all of us can benefit by pushing the "delay button" before we give our initial response to an emotional situation or encounter.

As a former district superintendent, or direct supervisor of clergy and churches, I would see some pastors fly off the handle in anger, and it produced those awkward moments of shock and silence by all who witnessed them. So the first level of emotional self-control is critical to our profession. We all know that there are disruptive emotions (anger, fear, hatred, lust, and so on) that usually fuel conflict rather than soothe or transform it, and these emotions are the ones that must be kept under control.

### Transparency

In some ways, the second dimension of self-management, transparency, almost sets up a contrary dilemma. Does not transparency mean that we share honestly what's on our hearts and minds? Well, yes and no. "Yes" to honest and deep sharing of what we are feeling and knowing, but "no" to knee-jerk emotional reactions that can distort what we mean almost immediately. Our role in ministry as "a professional" mitigates most emotional outbursts, and our training should mold our responses.

Where transparency makes such a difference in our spiritual leadership is when it enhances our perceived honesty, integrity, and trustworthiness. I say "perceived" because those of us who have integrity and honesty believe that it is true, but others do not know it without seeing and experiencing it for themselves. This strikes me every time we have to start a new ministry (whether it be a church, a role, or a new group in ministry). When you have been in ministry with a group for a long time and they know and trust you, your integrity is a given. However, when you start fresh with a whole new group of people who have not seen or experienced such integrity and trust, it takes time to earn it. You know you have it, but they do not. In such situations, it's easy to react with, "What do you mean, you don't trust me?"

I had spent less than a year as their new bishop when the appointed district superintendents and I were in the midst of making strategic plans. One of the more colorful superintendents blurted out: "We're not sure we trust you yet, Grant." My internal reaction was negative, as in "What do you mean you don't trust me!" Luckily, I hit the "delay button," and calmly responded, "I know I am new and trust needs to be earned."

The next year, in a similar context, I shared with this same group my internal reaction to that statement, and we all had a good laugh debriefing the first experience. By then transparency and trust had been developed to the point that we were able to share honestly about it and laugh at ourselves.

### Achievement and Initiative

Two of the other dimensions of self-management, achievement and initiative, speak directly about motivation. Achievement is defined as "the drive to improve performance to meet inner standards of excellence." This is a deeply valued martial arts concept. When you start any martial art as a beginner, you immediately see the skill level difference between yourself and the others with higher belt levels. It is a human tendency to compare oneself to others, and the motivation is to be like someone better. As you progress up the belt rankings, you learn that it is fruitless to compare yourself to others: there will always be greater and lesser skilled artists than yourself. If you have good instruction, a shift in value takes place: your performance is judged not against others, but internally, against oneself. You seek the perfect technique, which is always elusive, but a shift in competition lies in the change from an external comparison to an internal one.

Having learned this lesson as a young person in the martial arts, my motivation for excellence has always been internalized. I simply want to perform at the best level I can attain. Because ministry has its share of competition, there is a deep lesson here. I did not study this specific dimension of motivation in highly effective clergy, but I would guess when one reaches the mastery level of any art or profession, the basic motivation is internal, not external.

I have always been impressed with the broadness of leadership detailed in emotional intelligence, and initiative is one example. Initiative is defined as the "readiness to act and seize opportunities." In my research on highly effective clergy, I defined this quality as "entrepreneurial," and my operational definition was "immediately seizing on opportunities and avoiding hazards like the plague."

What I found interesting in the research is that many of the highly effective pastors had trouble with the word *entrepreneurial,* and the comments clustered around it being a word of the world (business especially). Some of these pastors chafed at the connotation, but when I defined it as "immediately seizing on opportunities and avoiding hazards like the plague," it was clear that they possessed this tendency.

Although the word "entrepreneur" was defined in the actual research question, as to reflect its applicability to the church setting, the business world has its own parameters for the word. The classical definition provided by economist Joseph Schumpeter (1883–1950) started with the fact that "entrepreneurs are not necessarily motivated by profit but regard it

as a standard for measuring achievement or success."[10] The qualities that Schumpeter attached to entrepreneurs: (a) greatly value self-reliance, (b) strive for distinction through excellence, (c) are highly optimistic (otherwise nothing would be undertaken), and (d) always favor challenges of medium risk (neither too easy, nor ruinous).[11]

In my research, using both the interview definition of an entrepreneur and Schumpeter's classical definition, highly effective UMC clergy did possess strong entrepreneurial behavior and skill sets. There is very little doubt that their success in ministry can be attributed to this entrepreneurial spirit and behavior.

One recent example comes from an urban church that was across the street from the site of thousands of striking public school teachers. Immediately seeing the needs, the pastor opened up the doors and bathrooms of the church to these teachers, inviting them in from the cold, and providing that tacit support that says, "we care about you." This action was a direct embodiment of "Open Hearts...Open Minds...Open Doors" (the United Methodist Church tagline), and for sure, these secular schoolteachers will remember the church's kindness and openness. It was also true that this pastor had to make an immediate response in order to seize upon this opportunity, and if he had felt compelled to get permission from the church board, the opportunity would have passed the church by. Leadership also means having the courage to venture forward, and to sometimes move ahead of the rules in order to take advantage of an opportunity.

Professional coach Lee Hayward would add the reflective art of "anticipation" to this mix. Taking the initiative to act without permission is fine, but highly effective clergy are able to anticipate what the resistance is going to be and prepare themselves for the possible fallout. This does involve measured risk-taking, but it is more in the form of anticipating what comes next from one's proactive initiative.[12]

## Adaptability and Optimism

Closely related to this situation is the quality of adaptability, which EQ defines as "flexibility in adapting to changing situations or overcoming obstacles." In opening up the church doors to those striking schoolteachers, that is exactly what the pastor practiced. Adaptability is one of the key themes of the new literature of adaptive leadership coming out of the Harvard Business School. The church is borrowing heavily from the adaptive leadership model, and I believe it is one of the most promising resources as

we head into an uncertain future. The very premise of adaptive leadership is that there are no answers currently available for adaptive problems, and no answers means there are no experts that we can turn to. Thus, the real work is placed on the shoulders of the people in the midst of the problem, as there are no road maps available, and experts do not have any real answers. Adaptive leaders must resist giving superficial answers and keep giving the experimental work back to the people themselves. Experimentation and risk-taking are at the core of the action taken in adaptive situations. The scope of this book will not allow for a detailed description and analysis of adaptive leadership, but the church needs to immerse itself in the literature, as I believe the principles will help us sort out our future. A short bibliography of adaptive leadership is included at the end of this chapter.

The final element of self-management is optimism, and this is always seeing the best and upside of any situation, person, or context. Optimism spreads enthusiasm, passion, and popularity, and there is a magnetic quality to leaders who are always looking at the bright side of all things.

Recently I observed an extremely strong and gifted spiritual leader process a very controversial issue with a group who was advocating one side of the issue. He clearly saw that this issue, if accepted, would be detrimental to the organization, and he had a clear negative opinion of the position that this group was advocating for. He professionally handled the processing of the issue, and objectively had the group look at both sides. He never exposed his own feelings about the issue, but worked through it with the group so that they could see some of the downsides. He never stopped being optimistic about the people and the future, but enabled them to weigh the decision in light of the whole community. In the end, he enabled this group to understand that they did not have the authority to make the decision, but they definitely felt heard and respected. However, it was his optimism about them and the future that was the deciding factor in a positive outcome. Even at the end of the meeting, he was smiling and joking with members of the group over relational insights into their lives and personalities.

## Social Awareness

### Empathy and Service

It is critical in emotional intelligence that we start with personal competence, as self-mastery leads to the second major area of emotional intelligence: social competence, or how we manage interpersonal relationships.

The first subdivision of social awareness is empathy, defined as "sensing others' emotions, understanding their perspective, and taking active interest in their concerns."

Empathy is usually a personal strength of clergy. It is something cultivated and developed throughout their ministerial career. In fact, many clergy go into ministry because of their interest in the primary care of others. Training and development in empathy is also one of the strengths of our seminary educational process, which excels in pastoral care and counseling as well as cinical pastoral education.

Closely aligned with empathy is EQ's category of service, which the researchers define as "recognizing and meeting follower, client, or customer needs." Once again, this is a personal strength of many clergy, but there can be unintended consequences as a result of clergy perhaps doing too good a job. The shadow side of service is that it can foster the consumerism side of ministry that mirrors a "professional to client" relationship. Instead of creating dynamic disciples who practice servant leadership to others, the therapeutic clergy model can foster a dependency on the minister who will take care of the parishioner. We have already addressed the downsides of this model previously. There is a place for authentic service in the Christian church, but it must be coupled with the parishioner's responsibility to be more than a passive recipient of services rendered by the minister.

Along with the theme of service it would be helpful to talk about the subject of servant leadership. The servant leadership model has greatly influenced Christian churches in America since its development in the late 1970s. Robert Greenleaf was the chief architect and spokesperson for the model, and he wrote and lectured extensively on the virtues of servant leadership throughout his adult life.

There is a natural affinity between the tenets of servant leadership and the biblical ethos of Jesus Christ in the New Testament. Many of the Synoptic Gospels recount Jesus modeling servant leadership and speaking of being a servant (Matt. 20:26ff; 25:31ff; Mark 9:35ff; John 13).

Ironically, Greenleaf would not accept that his idea of servant leadership came from the New Testament notion of "Whoever wishes to be great among you must be your servant..." (Matt. 20:26), but rather drew much of the ethos of servant leadership from the more Eastern religious story of Herman Hesse's *Journey to the East.*

Fundamentally, the servant leader serves one's subordinates by making them the priority and enabling the followers to achieve high standards and

greatness. The approach takes into account the larger community in the work environment, and posits that by demonstrating a servant's heart, the whole community will be uplifted to a higher sphere.

Servant leadership fundamentally counters the savior-hero leader, who single-handedly saves the day. Rather, the servant leader humbly empowers others to save the day, and is hardly noticed until she or he is missing. Servant leadership empowers and transforms—it does not control and dominate.

Researcher Larry Spears characterized the servant leader field by ten traits: listening, empathy, healing, awareness, persuasion, conceptualization, foresight, stewardship, commitment to the growth of people, and building a community.[13] Greenleaf himself was not a theologian by training but in fact was a secular AT&T employee and executive who crossed over in his writings from the business field to the nonprofit and religious world. Not fully understanding Greenleaf's stance, The United Methodist Church and other Christian denominations adopted his principles without depth of clarity. Thus, written into our UMC *Book of Discipline* as an expectation of all members: "for those persons to lead the church effectively, they must embody the teachings of Jesus in servant ministries and servant leadership."[14]

Indeed, the UMC *Book of Discipline* dedicates a special heading and paragraph just to servant leadership, and calls upon both laity and clergy to exemplify such behavior:

> Within The United Methodist Church, there are those called to servant leadership, lay and ordained. Such callings are evidenced by special gifts, evidence of God's grace, and promise of usefulness. God's call to servant leadership is inward as it comes to the individual and outward through the discernment and validation of the Church. The privilege of servant leadership in the Church is the call to share in the preparation of congregations and the whole Church for the mission of God in the world. The obligation of servant leadership is the forming of Christian disciples in the covenant community of the congregation. This involves discerning and nurturing the spiritual relationship with God that is the privilege of all servant ministers.[15]

Ordained ministers are called and set apart from the laity, but the burden of servant leadership for the role of clergy is especially pointed. The UMC

*Book of Discipline* explains:

> Ordained ministers are called by God to a lifetime of servant leadership in specialized ministries among the people of God.... The ordained ministry is defined by its faithful commitment to servant leadership following the example of Jesus Christ, by its passion for the hallowing of life, and by its concern to link all local ministries with the widest boundaries of the Christian community.[16]

What the UMC failed to recognize is that Greenleaf was adamantly opposed to the democratization of servant leadership, the rationale being that whole groups could not adequately carry out the tenents of servant leadership effectively.[17]

Greenleaf addressed this very issue in his own words:

> Twelve years ago when I wrote the first essay on *Servant as Leader* I discovered that I had given that piece a catchy title. I am grateful that the title gave the piece some circulation, but I am also aware of the danger servant leadership could become a gimmick. The top person of some ailing institution might try to insert servant leadership as a procedure, as a general management idea, as a means whereby the institution might do better. Such a move might have a short-lived aspirin effect, but when the effect wears off, it might leave the institution more ailing than it was before and another gimmick would need to be sought. The surer way for the idea to have a long-term effect *is for the top person to become a servant leader.* What that person *is* and *does* then speaks louder than what is said. It might be better if nothing is said, just *be* it. This, in time, might transform the institution.[18]

Greenleaf's caution here has been a self-fulfilling prophecy for The United Methodist Church. Much like Edgar Schein's "espoused beliefs and values,"[19] the church has paid lip service to the value while not exemplifying it in actual practice.

It is a fact that most organizations attempt to maintain a homeostasis by reinforcing structures, elevating leaders, and maintaining stability through the status quo. The organized church does not escape this process.

It has been my experience as a bishop in the UMC with the expressed role as the "spiritual and temporal leader of the church" that quite contrary to the expectation for the highest office in the church to live out servant leadership, quite the opposite is the case. Bishops are generally treated with a deference not of servant but of king or queen. Bishops are given the best service, rooms, and means of transportation. Often, when visiting local churches as the bishop my attempt to exercise the role of servant by serving people, cleaning up, or physically helping out is met with resistance from the laity by their saying, "you shouldn't be doing that." Following Greenleaf's intention, I resist giving in and try to model that servant behavior as a way to send a visual message to the clergy and laity. However, the resistance to servant leadership in the actual practices of the church should be noted and prophetically challenged on a regular basis.

This leads to another deep-seated systemic constraint of The United Methodist Church, and perhaps other denominations: namely, the culture of entitlement over service in ministry. With the professionalization of ministry in North America and the setting aside of full-time vocationally compensated clergy members, a culture of entitlement over service has crept into our clergy orders. It works in two ways, one for the clergy and one for the laity of local churches. As it plays out for clergy, there is a built-in expectation of a livable salary and accompanying benefits for full-time ministry. Because The United Methodist Church currently has a guarantee of full-time ministry employment for life in its polity, there is the expectation of that entitlement by the clergy. As it applies to the laity, there is the built-in expectation that each local church will receive a full-time minister, even if they cannot sustain the cost of that minister. This expectation is often passed off to the annual conference or judicatory to close the necessary funding gap in order to secure one minister for each local charge. When the local church and judicatory cannot afford to provide for a full-time minister for a local church, the options of less than full-time or linking two or three churches in close proximity becomes the realistic option. However, there is the hope that such churches will regain the membership strength to go back to a full-time minister. The entitlement mentality is reinforced on each side of this issue. Returning to a true servant leadership model would mean that both clergy and laity would see ministry as gift rather than entitlement, and behave accordingly. If all of us started by first engaging in ministry for the sheer love of God and neighbor alone, entitlement would not be the problem that it is today. However, with professionalized ministry, laity expectations of one minister for each local church, and a large and endowed pension plan for the church, entitlement has become embedded

in the fabric of the church culture itself. We know superficial fixes will not work, as deep culture change is the only possibility for dealing with this systemic constraint.

### Organizational Awareness

As much as clergy are trained in the empathy-service side of ministry, the opposite is probably true of the other dimension of social awareness: organizational awareness, which is defined as "reading the currents, decision networks, and politics at the organizational level." Clearly, this is not a strength or major concern of most seminary curriculums, although some seminary programs are taking this quite seriously. Garrett-Evangelical Seminary's "Ministry Plus" program has partnered with Northwestern Business School to provide specialized classes to recent graduates who are out in the field. The brilliance of this program is that it provides the practical organizational knowledge to new working practitioners who need it the most.

However, new clergy in their first appointments who have not had the luxury of this type of program are usually ill-equipped to deal with the organizational side of the church, unless they have had business or secular training in their past. It is here that the church must step in and provide the needed practical understanding of organizational life for new ministers. Judicatory committees who deal with ministerial candidates or newly ordained clergy in their probation period are key providers of specialized organizational training for inexperienced clergy practitioners.

When I took my first full-time appointment I was twenty-six years old, and had not taken one business course through high school or college. Luckily, I did have an entrepreneurial spirit, having opened a small business with my sister when we were both in college. However, I had not worked in or experienced a large organizational system in my entire life. My first appointment was to a family-sized church, so I did not immediately need the knowledge of how to work with a large and complex system. Yet, seminary did not prepare me to understand some of the basics of organizational development: how decisions are made, the politics of roles and of power, how one can enable things to get done, and so on. There were also the myriad of other larger denominational administrative tasks: annual reports of statistical information, budgeting and apportionment payments (the United Methodist church's financial obligation to the denomination), and a stream of administrative forms and reports.

Although I had a strong intuitive grasp of finances, I never learned

beforehand how to run a stewardship campaign or effective nonprofit fundraiser. Seminary did not teach about putting together annual budgets for the church, or how to develop endowments or deferred giving. Even the ultra practical "How to buy a copying machine for the office" would have been appropriate for that first year of ministry. I also needed a crash course on church repairs and construction, as I was appointed to a church with an older building.

In other words, there were hundreds of practical, day-to-day ministry activities that were constant but for which I was not specifically trained. I realized that in those first few years of solo ministry, one has to be resourceful, and much learning is based on trial and error.

I also sought out resources and training on my own. One of the most helpful courses was a nonprofit fundraising course that led to a certification in nonprofit stewardship. During those early years of ministry, almost everything I learned about stewardship came out of that program.

I now see what would be extremely helpful for clergy who are right out of seminary and taking their first church appointment would be a series of practical seminars and workshops with basic "how to" information. I would couple this with peer learning groups that share best practices in light of these basic local church issues. New pastors would then go back to their local church assignments, trying out new materials and processes to see what does and does not work. Using the local church as a living laboratory, and debriefing the experiments with other peers by sharing case studies and results, would thus accelerate learning.

However, the model of peer learning groups should not be confined to those who are just starting their ministry. Facing adaptive challenges, all of us in the ministry need to be in peer learning groups in order to learn from and with each other. Adaptive change means that there are no road maps or guides available. We have to continue to forge new ministry experiments and see what works within our specific ministry contexts.

## Social Competence: Relationship Management

The final EQ category is relationship management, and once again, it is impressive to see the breadth of leadership qualities inherent in this area. At the top of this list is inspirational leadership, which is defined as "guiding and motivating with a compelling vision."

So much of the secular literature on leadership revolves around the

twin principles of "inspiration" and "vision." The language of leadership should be inspiration, and the truly great leaders have the ability to inspire followers to reach heights that they normally would not be able to achieve. Inspiration is often linked to charisma, but that devolves leadership back to the old days of the "Great Man" theory that leaders are born, not made. There is no doubt that there are charismatic leaders, but much of the research shows that the quality of charisma is not a guarantee for sustained success. Jim Collins's work on "level 5 leaders" shows that those leaders who have produced sustained levels of greatness for their organizations are not charismatic at all. Rather, they possess a humbleness that mitigates charisma, but also a fierce resolve to take their organization to the top. In fact, charisma can work in the opposite direction of organizational greatness, as those who possess it often have an egocentricity that motivates people to follow them, not the organization. So, the lesson here is that inspiration should always be directed toward the church, not the leader.

The second insight about inspiration is that the best mode or practice of it comes through story. Inspirational story should be the language of the spiritual leader. Since narrative is our theologically preferred mode, we have a natural advantage over secular business. Clergy have been trained in preaching and communications, and weaving story into all of our communications is by no means a stretch for us. People are inspired by stories, and there is a natural affinity we have for the narrative mode and practice.

From a major Gallup survey of what followers are looking for from a leader is the ability to create hope. Other words mentioned by followers about their leaders were "direction, faith, and guidance."[20] These are all Christian church–based words, and the secular world has co-opted these words from us for their own purposes. We need to reclaim these words in our own leadership, and probably the single most important quality that we offer the church of the present is hope and inspiration.

Vision is also one of the natural foundations that business has borrowed from the church. Historically, the church has always attempted to follow the greater vision of God, and the church has suffered without divine vision or when human vision replaces that of God. Vision is also the work of the people, not necessarily the leader alone. When the leader alone sets the vision, it is subject to the all too human prejudices that creep into it. So, any vision has to be confirmed by the people of God, who will be the final judge to its authenticity and ability to compel.

There is nothing wrong with leaders projecting their vision, but they have to understand that it cannot be their vision alone; in order to be effective, the people have to respond to the vision in a positive way and own it as theirs. What leaders can do is to listen deeply to what the people envision as their preferred future, synthesize that vision into a compelling narrative, and test to see if it captures what they have been saying. Leaders thus play a vital role in vision making, but ultimately the people must appropriate the vision and own it.

## Influence

Another huge dimension of relationship management is influence. The EQ researchers define influence as "wielding a range of tactics for persuasion." One would think that influence would be an absolute "must" quality of Christian ministers, as the faith is only transmitted through our persuasion of others of its truth.

A full quantitative analysis needs to be done using StrengthsFinder to assess if, in general, clergy do not possess this signature strength. If true, this fact would have profound impact on the effective work of spiritual leaders. I know I personally do not possess the influencer strength, and this has as much to do with my cultural background as any other factor. As a third-generation Asian American, I have been brought up with the notion that you should not stand out but rather blend in with others. The old Asian cultural adage is "the nail that sticks up gets hammered down." Both nuclear family as well as my Asian American community values have shaped my personality in this particular way.

The perfect illustration of this is in the StrengthsFinder quality of "woo," or the ability to influence others around you in a persuasive way. I was taught that in large gatherings of people, you should blend in with others, but the influencer quality means that you need to "work" the room by going up to others and introducing yourself and networking. In these situations I have to reach outside my comfort zone to make contacts and meet a wide variety of people. This reinforces the truth that leadership can be learned, and by reaching outside our comfort zones, we can stretch in new ways for growth and development. Anybody can do this. It may not be natural, but we can all stretch ourselves in new and dynamic ways.

To emphasize that growth in leadership involves stretching outside our comfort zones, I created the following diagram, influenced by concepts in Geoff Colvin's *Talent Is Overrated*:

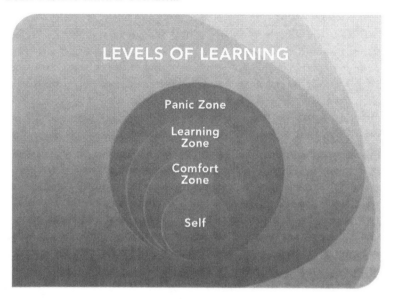

Everyone has a natural comfort zone in which they are most at ease, but true learning takes place at the level just outside one's comfort zone. It is the stretching beyond what is comfortable that enables one to grow stronger. Exercise in human physiology is the perfect example. If I am weight training and desire to grow stronger, then I need to increase the weight lifted incrementally, in order for a muscle to tear and then repair itself. In this process, the muscle grows larger and thus stronger. If I lift the same weight without ever increasing the total amount of weight lifted, I may maintain my present strength and size, but I will not grow stronger. However, if I lift too much weight, I run the risk of damaging a muscle or bone beyond its ability to repair itself, and will actually harm my body in the process. This is what happens when I move outside the learning zone into the panic zone. I am not able to handle the total weight, or the pressure of the experience itself, and I end up harming myself, or others.

Obviously, knowing the limits of these zones is critical. If one is new to weight training or ministry, having an experienced trainer or mentor is a must. An athletic trainer will be able to tell you how much weight you should attempt to lift and even have a training regiment for you to follow.

Likewise, an experienced mentor in the ministry can reflect honestly with you about your current expectations and limits, and tell you when you need to stretch outside your comfort zone into the learning zone and when to avoid doing too much and entering the panic zone.

Leadership kaizen also makes a huge difference in teaching you not to undertake so much as to enter the panic zone. Slow, steady improvement is the foundation of spiritual leadership growth, and moving out of one's comfort zone in small steps is certainly preferable to a huge leap that just may push one into the panic zone.

### Change Catalyst

Another huge dimension of relationship management is being a change catalyst, which is defined as "initiating, managing, and leading in a new direction." It must be clear that we have to reset our ministry paradigm, and to do so involves changing the church at almost every level. I would say that most of my work at the annual conference level and above has been about change management. I have also observed that unless the top authority figures are committed to deep change, it will not happen. Here, existing organizational structures are extremely resistant to change. Organizations are designed for homeostasis, or seeking the optimum balance of stability. To disrupt this stasis is to cause the system to be in anxiety, and the pull is always back to the point of past stability that the organization has always known. Unless the top authority of the organization is willing to risk the destabilizing of the organization, and align all of the other leaders toward the change agenda, very little change will happen. I have made many attempts at changing a United Methodist annual conference (as a clergy member, leader of a transitions team, and a district superintendent), but I have been able to leverage so much more as a bishop of an annual conference. Because bishops are the spiritual and temporal leaders of annual conferences, there is a persuasive power that we hold in making necessary changes. The United Methodist Church Discipline (the polity and rules of the UMC) does not give bishops wide executive powers (except to appoint clergy), but even still we wield a great deal of influence in the life of the church.

Thus, the top leadership of the church must want and work for change, or else the forces of resistance will be too strong for anything significant to happen. For clergy of local churches this means that the change process starts with you, and you must put the entire weight of your office and role behind the change. You must also enlist your top lay leaders, and align the whole church behind the change initiatives.

Understanding the change process is also critical. Clergy need to study the literature about change (what the effects are), and also the process of change (how to do it). William Bridges provides the best psychological understanding of change when he points out that the word *change* describes the actual circumstances of the change, but *transitions* points to the emotional reactions of those undergoing the change. Most of the minefields involve the transitions that people go through when experiencing change. Change as reflected in people's transitions (emotional reactions) produces anxiety and conflict. Conflict is a natural byproduct of transitions, and good leadership is prepared to deal with such conflict.

## Conflict Management

This leads naturally into another dimension of relationship management, which is conflict management, defined simply as "resolving disagreements." The leadership chain here is rather simple: Being a change catalyst produces transitions conflict, and a good leader then provides conflict management. Clearly, we are talking here of a specific skill set, and if the spiritual leader learns the basics of conflict management and resolution, it will put her or him ahead of the curve. To supplement their reading and research on conflict management, I would suggest clergy take an intensive workshop on the subject. The church has many valuable resources available on conflict transformation and resolution, and workshops are readily available. If at all possible, take those workshops that allow participants to role-play and practice various conflict resolution techniques. Being a skill set, conflict management is best learned through practice, and the more experience one has in conflict situations the better prepared one becomes.

## Building Bonds

The last three relationship management issues are distinct yet interrelated in an iterative way. The first one to examine is building bonds, which is defined as "cultivating and maintaining a web of relationships." One of the hallmarks of resetting our ministry involves reaching out to the postmodern generations. Although each of the generations is unique and different from the others, they share some common generalities. One of these is "high tech," or the fact that overall younger people are more computer and internet savvy than previous generations. This fact has fundamentally changed how the attractional church model works, as young adults will not just drop by to visit your church. Overall, their entry point is the internet, and if they are interested in looking for a church at all, they will surf elec-

tronically and seek out the church's website. Well-designed websites are a plus, as young adults also want to navigate your website to find out what is offered. Since pure affiliation with any institution is not a priority, there is usually a specific program or interest that they are searching for. In general, younger people are not interested in an insular community setting, but hope to be involved with something that is making a tangible difference in the neighborhood, community, or greater society and world. If we are to attract the younger generations, our churches must also be involved missionally beyond themselves.

So, the entry point is "high tech," but the staying point is "high touch," or the fact that there must be a strong sense of relationship building if younger folks are to stay connected with a local church. Here is something that our Christian churches both understand and can excel at. Relationship building has been at the core of our ministry for thousands of years, and if we can capitalize on this sense of community building, we have a shot at attracting younger generations.

The leadership task of building bonds, or cultivating and maintaining a web of relationships, becomes critical to our ministry. If we are to attract younger generations the mode of our relationship building must also change to reflect a more "high tech" approach. Currently, there are some young adult ministries that communicate solely by social networking. Some of these ministries do not have permanent locations, so they will text or Facebook a date, time, and location a day or so ahead, and people will just show up. For those with large followings, their worship experience and community building is first class, so there is motivation to attend. However, this breaks all the traditional church rules about communications, and it demonstrates how the mode of maintaining a web of relationship is changing.

The dilemma of attracting younger generations highlights the need for a hybrid system between the traditional "attractional" model and the new "missional" model of reaching out into the mission field directly. The above example of a social networking church fits this hybrid description perfectly.

### Developing Others: A Discipling System

One pronounced weakness of many of our mainline local churches is the lack of a comprehensive and compelling disciplining system, or a way for people to grow deeper in their faith, and thus remain interested in attending the church. This speaks directly to the relationship management

element of developing others, which the EQ researchers define as "bolstering others' abilities through feedback and guidance." Obviously, this definition refers more directly to a secular workplace environment, and this is an important skill set for clergy who are part of a multiple staff arrangement. But the even greater applicability to the church is the fact that a healthy discipling system for laity provides for the spiritual development of the congregation in a systemic and holistic way. Thus, transposing a discipling definition to developing others comes out simply: "bolstering others' spiritual lives through feedback and guidance."

Even though U.S. society is growing increasingly secular and not looking for religious affiliation, this does not mean that people are becoming less spiritually inclined. In fact, there is a growing trend to seek spiritual meaning through both new age materials and interfaith exploration. I have a Buddhist colleague who oversees a fairly large Japanese American Buddhist Temple in the Los Angeles area, and his largest influx of newcomers are non–Japanese American seekers who are looking for spiritual meaning. He regularly jokes that his Temple is the most unfriendly one in the area, as he is interested in serious Buddhists, and not fair-weather seekers.

Another growing trend is spirituality in the workplace, which is drawing increasing interest from both employees and employers wishing to create a more productive workplace environment. Historically, spirituality related to religion has been a taboo subject for businesses, but enlightened employers are looking to establish more productive working conditions for their employees, and if spirituality has the potential to increase morale and productivity, then some find it welcome. An important point is that spirituality in the workplace does not mean any particular faith tradition, and in fact strives for the non-partisan approach to religion itself.

Whereas traditionally one sought out a local church for spiritual exploration, that is no longer the case in our present time. As fewer churches are offering a safe and relevant atmosphere to explore one's deepest questions about life, meaning, and faith, the public is seeking this function in other arenas, including the secular marketplace of new age materials.

What this means to the mainline church is that we must recover the function of spiritual discovery in a relevant and nonthreatening way. A healthy discipling system does this very thing, as small groups and classes seek to explore and develop one's individual faith. As spiritual leaders, our task is to develop the spiritual lives of our parishioners, as we give feedback and guidance.

### Teamwork and Collaboration

The final dimension of relationship management is teamwork and collaboration, defined simply as "fostering cooperation and team building." Any experienced spiritual leader is well acquainted with this skill, as pulling together a volunteer organization like the local church relies on cooperation and team building.

I will be speaking of the whole skill set of cooperation and collaboration in the next area, transformational leadership, but let me touch lightly on the theme of team building. As mentioned previously, I think one of the hardest role transitions for clergy is when they move from a pastoral-size church to a larger, program sized church. In my experience, many clergy are not able to adapt from the pastoral-size role when they are appointed or called to the larger church size. When clergy cannot reinvent themselves from the pastoral mentality, the local church rubber bands back to the pastoral size where the clergy is in his or her comfort zone. A simple example: a pastor moves from a pastoral-size church (150 average in worship) to a program-size church (250 average in worship) and insists on doing and leading everything like he or she used to in the previous church. Whereas the program-size church utilized ministry teams to carry on the larger programmatic role, the new minister insists on being involved in and overseeing everything. This produces the "pastoral bottleneck syndrome," as everything grinds to a halt to allow it to go through one person. Ministry teams get discouraged, as authority and responsibility are usurped from laity to pastor. Whereas with 150 people the pastor was able to manage such direct involvement, it becomes impossible with 250 people. Gifted lay leaders become discouraged and pull back from their volunteer commitments. The more the pastor tries to dominate the ministry, the more people drift away, and pretty soon, the church is back to the pastoral size of an average of 150 people in its primary worship service.

Many clergy who cannot adapt to a new role in ministry simply do not see these dynamics, and lacking the EQ quality of self-management, fail to do ministry in a new way. Oftentimes, they double their effort and workload in an attempt to take on more, and at the same time this makes the problem worse by driving away more dedicated laity.

By practicing the final component of team building, pastoral-dominated clergy can move to a new orientation in their ministry. Team building means that you trust the team over yourself, and do not engage in solo leadership. Instead of taking on the responsibility of everything them-

selves, clergy move to the role of resourcing and empowering the laity to do the work of ministry. Through the creation of multiple teams, more ministry can be accomplished, and more people can be directly involved. Once again, inspiration becomes key, as the pastor's role is not direct leadership, but inspiring lay leaders to greater involvement.

It is imperative to emphasize that merely practicing team building will not make a difference if pastors cannot reinvent themselves out of the pastoral-size mentality. There must be the individual change commitment to do ministry in an intentionally different way. Here, any pastor serving a church that is growing to the next size transition needs to understand what the pastoral role is at the next larger size and begin to model that type of behavior. Be sure to take a look at the recommended bibliography on church size transitions to study how the role of the pastor must change with different size churches.

It turns out that the number of 150 is not an arbitrary figure but has much scientific backing. Malcolm Gladwell points this out in the research of the British anthropologist Robin Dunbar. Dunbar's theory, called "social channel capacity," equates brain size to the size of the primary group one belongs to. His conclusion for primates: the larger the neocortex of the brain, the larger the average size of the group they live in.

The basis of the theory is that as our brains evolve, the neocortex increases in size that must be due to the larger social connections. Dunbar uses the argument that if you belonged to a group of five people, you must keep track of ten separate relationships: your four direct relationships, and six other two-way relationships among the rest of the group. If you increase the size of the group to, say, twenty people, then the numbers grow exponentially: nineteen direct relationships with yourself, and 171 possible relationships that the group members have with one another.

For clergy, there is a constant juggling of relational information to track: Judy's mother is in the hospital; Janice's child is having trouble at school; Bob's marriage is going through some tough times, not to mention all of the other relationship entanglements that clergy get drawn into. Mary doesn't work well with Joan, because her daughter can't stand her son; Tom is too laid back and can't be paired with Bob, who is a task-master supreme on this church project; Gwen needs to be assigned with her best friend Carol in order to commit to this assignment; and so on. Clergy know this litany of personal relationships by heart!

As Gladwell concludes:

> Humans socialize in the largest groups of all primates be-
> cause we are the only animals with brains large enough to
> handle the complexities of that social arrangement. Dunbar
> has actually developed an equation, which works for most
> primates, in which he plugs in what he calls the neocortex
> ratio of a particular species—the size of the neocortex rela-
> tive to the size of the brain—and the equation spits out the
> expected maximum group size of the animal. If you plug in
> the neocortex ratio for Homo sapiens, you get a group esti-
> mate of 147.8—or roughly 150. The figure of 150 seems to
> represent the maximum number of individuals with whom
> we can have a genuinely social relationship, the kind of re-
> lationship that goes with knowing who they are and how
> they relate to us. Putting it in another way, it's the number
> of people you would not feel embarrassed about joining un-
> invited for a drink if you happened to bump into them in
> a bar.[21]

As a result of studying the anthropological literature, Dunbar finds that the number 150 remains constant in studies that track the limit to our natural ability to stand in fairly close relationship with others. It also happens to be the limit of how many people a minister can serve as the center of the pastoral size role. As the congregation grows beyond this point, the pastor simply cannot keep track of that many relationships and must give up trying to be the center of everything. If one fails to do so it means that the church will be locked into the number 150 and not grow beyond that point.

I have always been impressed with the comprehensive list of leadership qualities that emotional intelligence supports. If you are like me, you probably never thought EQ involved such qualities as achievement, influence, inspiration, and being a change catalyst. It is for this reason that I believe every spiritual leader should be willing to work on emotional intelligence on a regular basis. One can grow stronger in EQ, and through quantitative research we have established it as a fundamental requirement of high effectiveness in ministry. For further study of EQ, please refer to the bibliography.

# Do This, Not That!

The comprehensiveness and complexity of what is included in emotional intelligence means that a spiritual leader must prioritize what to concentrate and work on. Trying to take on too much will lead to failure. My prescriptive advice is to look at the list from Goleman, as cited earlier in this chapter, and decide on one or two areas to concentrate on. These don't necessarily have to be perceived areas of weakness, for remember the Strengths-Finder's philosophy that we should maximize our strengths and manage our weaknesses. Working on your emotional intelligence means prioritization first, and with so many categories, it may become a lifelong process.

Spiritual leadership kaizen also reinforces our making a slow but steady improvement over a lifetime of ministry.

# The Third of the Big Three: Transformational Leadership

The final element in my "big three" of spiritual leadership is transformational leadership. I am almost tempted to use another title than "transformational leadership," as this title has been overused, and people often do not have a precise definition of it. However, I am attracted to the word "transformational," as it embodies the spiritual purpose of my own life and work in many ways.

While doing my coursework for the EdD program in Organizational Leadership at Pepperdine University, I was assigned to come up with a short elevator speech. Elevator speeches are very short descriptions of who you are and what you do in life, and they are patterned after what you might say to a stranger in a short elevator ride (one to two minutes in length). For example, if you got to ride on an elevator with President Obama, and he asked you who you are, what would you say?

Actually, it would be more realistic if the question came from the Secret Service agents, but having a response you had already thought about would be helpful. I hate doing these kinds of exercises, but for a grade, I had to participate. My elevator speech goes like this:

"My name is Grant Hagiya (smile), and my lifelong ambition is to help transform lives so that those lives can transform communities, and thus the world. I love dark chocolate, any sport with a ball in it, and deep provocative ideas that make me stop and think."

Now, would I ever recite that to President Obama? Probably not. But if asked, I would affirm my commitment to transform lives and the world—thus, my attraction to the word "transformational." It is also the fundamental mission statement of the United Methodist Church: "We are to make disciples of Jesus Christ for the transformation of the world."

Some of us would like to transpose the mission statement to read: "For the transformation of the world, we are to make disciples of Jesus Christ." This simple transposition represents how some people became disciples of Jesus Christ, namely by a commitment to social justice and change, or the importance that God places first on a transformed spiritual world. I am good with the mission statement either way.

## Defining Transformational Leadership

In defining transformation leadership, we might look at its opposite: transactional leadership, which is expressed in a mutual exchange of goods or services. It is exemplified in the phrase "give for get," as each person gives and receives something in return. In a business sense, transactional leadership is expressed in the paternalistic notion that management provides wages and benefits to the employees, who give back in their hard work and loyalty to the company.

As practical as this notion seems, it runs counter to the Gospel message of extravagant grace, a contrast best exemplified in the Synoptic story of the laborers in the vineyard who work all day, and yet the laborers who come only in the last hour to work are paid the same full day's wage as all others. When those who worked the whole day protest, the response is that they received exactly what they contracted for and ought not question the owner's generosity to give an equal share to all. Such extravagant grace is the transforming power of God in Jesus Christ.

Thus, as Christians we believe not in a transactional relationship with others but in a transformational one in which the divine grace of God is modeled and shared. If we think in terms of needs, a transactional relationship facilitates a mutual exchange to fulfill both parties' needs. However, a transformational relationship acknowledges that alone, I do not have enough to fulfill my needs, and you do not have enough to fulfill your own needs, but perhaps together we can pool our resources and power to fulfill both our needs. Thus, a transformation happens in both of us as we collaborate to better our communal situation. If we think in terms of a larger com-

munity, all of us should work for transformation of ourselves, each other, and the larger good of the whole.

Still, this example above falls short of the divine grace of God. The Wesleyan paradigm of personal piety is helpful here. Once I acknowledge my sinful nature, repent, and seek transformation from this sin, I enter into the state of justification. It is the acknowledgement that I am saved by the divine grace of God alone. In justification I am saved from the guilt of sin, and restored to the favor of God.

As I continue on my spiritual journey, I enter the state of sanctification, and here I am saved from the power and root of sin, and I am restored to the image of God. My motivation remains consistent, as I realize I live and am saved because God loves me unconditionally. I cannot earn this love, but it is freely given simply because I am a child of God. So in my quest through sanctification, my love of God and neighbor grows ever deeper. My personal self is often eclipsed in this quest of love of God and neighbor. In business terms, this is not a zero-sum game, whereby there will only be enough love for a few, and choices have to be made. God's love flows abundantly and continually to all. Wesley called this love "prevenient grace," and it is infinite in its output and depth. My personal realization that God loves me with the depth of unconditional love like this has transformed my life, and put its own spin on what it means to practice transformational leadership.

So as spiritual leaders, we practice transformational leadership far beyond the secular notion of this style. Even as I share the secular definition of transformational leadership, we would do well to remember the depth of transformation we seek as spiritual leaders.

According to researchers Bernard Bass and Bruce Avolio, transformational leadership has four components:

- Charismatic role modeling

- Inspirational motivation

- Intellectual stimulation

- Individualized consideration[22]

Leaders who have a specific vision and a high ethical standard that followers subscribe to and wish to emulate would be described as demonstrating charisma. Charismatic leaders have strong convictions, high self-confidence, and a tendency to dominate and influence others.[23]

The second factor, "inspirational motivation," occurs when a leader builds a team through communication and inspiration of a shared vision. "What is necessary for leaders, whether regarded as charismatic or transformational, is that they have a compelling vision and that they find a way to communicate it."[24]

The third factor, "intellectual stimulation," is manifest when a leader demonstrates supportive behavior in challenging followers by innovation and problem solving. As stated by researchers Masood, Dani, Burns, and Backhouse, "transformational leaders raise the consciousness of the followers with ideals, morals and values while not subscribing to negative emotions such as fear or greed."[25]

The final factor the leader uses is "individualized consideration." This is characterized by the development of followers in coaching or mentoring them to reach individual fulfillment. To quote researcher Constant Beugre and associates: "In addition to providing inspirational motivation and intellectual stimulation, transformational leaders provide individualized consideration to followers, showing respect and dignity and serving as mentors."[26]

In my own research, highly effective UMC clergy demonstrated all four of these components in their leadership and ministry. Let's take a closer look at some specific examples.

## Charismatic Role Modeling

Charisma is a very nebulous concept, and we tend to operate out of stereotypes of it rather than specific operational definitions. Researchers Bernard Bass and Bruce Avolio help us tremendously when they provide this definition: "leaders who have a specific vision and a high ethical standard that followers subscribe to and wish to emulate."[27] We have already talked about vision, but a high ethical standard should be an "absolute must" for spiritual leaders. In my mind, high ethical standards lead naturally to a sense of integrity, where our inner compass of what is right always matches our outer behaviors. The overused slogan "walk the talk" is supplanted with "walk the mark," and that mark is personal integrity.

One of the supreme examples of ethical leadership that I have known is John Wooden, UCLA's legendary basketball coach. I had met Coach Wooden a couple of times through a close friend of his, and he even helped out in a charity event of the local church that I was serving. In addition, I had the once-in-a-lifetime opportunity to conduct a one-on-one inter-

view with Coach Wooden for a leadership project. He was the epitome of a leader in so many ways, but my main impression of him was as supreme ethical leader. For example, the interview with Coach Wooden was part of an academic class that I was in, and there were strict guidelines that we had to follow in order to protect the rights and safety of those we would interview. Universities have an internal review board (IRB) that governs the policies and procedures of any interview or experiment with live subjects. In going over the IRB policy guidelines (a long list of legally crafted words) with him before the interview, John didn't bother to read the paper; he just signed his name on the sheet. I asked him, "John, are you sure you don't want to reread these policies?" He shook his head and was ready to move on. Our mutual friend who was present and had set up the interview was also surprised, and commented, "John trusts you." It was a small yet revealing example of his ethical character.

Northouse mentions five principles of ethical leadership: "Respects others, serves others, shows justice, manifests honesty, and builds community."[28] John Wooden lived these principles and demonstrated them daily in his coaching and teaching career. In his own words, he lays the foundation of his ethical leadership stance:

> I have always said that your character...you're the only one who really knows your character. Your reputation is what you are perceived to be by others...it is not necessarily what you really are, it could be, but it isn't necessarily so, but your character is what you really are and you are the only one that knows that, and in the long run you should definitely be more concerned about your character than your reputation.[29]

As to the qualities of ethical leadership that Northouse outlines, it was so clear how much John cared for his players:

> I wanted my basketball players to know that I cared for them, not just as basketball players, but I cared for them as individuals. I wanted to know all about them, all I could find out. I would let them know that I was interested in their brothers and sisters, their parents, their problems, their joys and their sorrows. I wanted to know all about them that I could, and help give a better line on how I could work with certain individuals.

Northouse's other quality of respect for others was also a strong emphasis of Coach Wooden:

> You have to study and analyze each individual recognizing that they are all different. They come from different backgrounds...different size...different appearance...maybe different religions...maybe different politics. I don't care what your race is, what your religion is, what your politics are. Have something, and stand up for it, but stay open-minded, listen to the other fellow—that's the main thing, to stay open minded.

Throughout the interview Coach Wooden talked about justice as fairness, and the need to treat everyone fairly. Here, he modeled the dimension of "showing justice." Over dinner he commented that he thought women basketball players played the game at a more pure form than the men. His commitment to justice can also be seen in his perspective of the women's game:

> For example, in the WNBA, how many women head coaches are there? Not too many. Yet, I am sure that many women are just as capable as the men. I find in the collegians, I think we have probably, I believe as many, or many more women coaching winning teams than men. But there are no women coaching the men's teams, but there are still a lot of men coaching the women's teams. I would say as Title 9 has come into effect, and the years have gone by, the gap is closing. It is a slow process, but it is closing. As many other things in life, the race isn't as wide as it was. Is it where it should be? No. Has it been closing? Yes, it is much closer than it was.

Coach Wooden's whole basketball philosophy was built on playing as a team. He exemplified the notion of "building community," and simply would not tolerate placing individual performance above team performance. Here is how he put it in the interview:

> It is my job to try getting that individual building to work for the team as a whole—for the group as a whole. But your job is to try to improve yourself individually to the best of your ability, and my job is to try to get you to not only...do the

things that will help you improve, but to get you to do that for the welfare of the group, not just for yourself.

The final quality I want to mention about Coach Wooden was his deep and abiding faith. He never stated that his ethical stance came from his faith, but they were inextricably bound together. I believe he would have made a great minister, although the world would have been robbed of one of the greatest coaches of all time.

One parenthetical note that Coach Wooden had on the concept of kaizen: he believed in it completely in the development of his players. As he commented:

> To get it across to them that my expectations are that they do not try to be better than somebody else, but that each day they must try to improve themselves a little. I tried to get that across to them: try to improve a little each day. Don't expect to improve a lot, but a little, and as the days go by, that little each day will soon amount to quite a bit.

Sage advice from one of the greatest coaches who ever lived!

## Intellectual Stimulation

We have talked extensively about the second factor of "inspirational motivation," in our discussion about inspiration and vision, so let's take a look at the third factor, which Bass and Avolio describe as "intellectual stimulation." In some ways, this is a misnamed title, as the definition of this transformational quality is to raise the leadership level of followers through innovation and problem solving, two very corporate examples. For spiritual leaders, the Masood definition is more fruitful: "transformational leaders raise the consciousness of the followers with ideals, morals and values while not subscribing to negative emotions such as fear or greed."

I once studied for a short while with a Gung-fu master whose style of teaching consisted of short bursts of demonstrated technique. In other words, he did not verbally teach the students by talking to us, but rather, every once in a while, he would physically demonstrate a technique with precision and grace. It took me a while to get used to this pedagogical form, as for much of the lesson time the students were on their own to work on

the techniques of this style. But I must say, when he did demonstrate to us in this fashion, it inspired us to emulate his mastery of the art.

In many ways at the local church, our spiritual leaders inspire us through preaching, teaching, and pastoral care. They act as role models for us, and we are inspired by the raising of our consciousness to a higher level. In fact, that is exactly my goal in my own classroom teaching: to raise the reflective consciousness of the students through inspiration of lofty visions and ideals. In an academic environment, it is the provocative ideas that seem to do this best, and the greater the degree of provocation the more dramatic the effect. An example is those authors whose first book and landmark ideas provoke a strong response in their fields. As the critics hammer on the margins of their ideas, bright authors evolve their ideas to a less risky middle ground. Very seldom is the author's second book on the same subject as provocative and risky as the first venture.

This same principle might apply to spiritual leaders in local churches. Bland preaching and teaching very seldom move me. It is when the preacher provokes me intellectually, emotionally, or spiritually that something churns inside of my heart and head. Such provocation can be either positive or negative. In other words, I can be provoked because I have affinity with the position being advocated or if I disagree with the position. The point is that I am moved out of my comfort zone, and stimulated to act or respond.

Personally, I prefer to be provoked, even negatively, than to be subjected to a safe and comfortable sermon or lesson. I am most troubled by bland and cautious sermons or Bible studies. To be inspired or disgusted is preferable to no reaction at all. If our objective is transformation, I will only get there by someone pushing me out of my comfort zone to a place that I may or may not wish to go. I simply will not get there by something that is safe and cautious!

Jesus continued to do this throughout his ministry, and as modern biblical scholarship has shown, Jesus represented the radical prophetic tradition as much as any other of the roles that he assumed. He called into radical question the religious, economic, and political systems of his time, and he was killed because of his courage and prophetic witness.

In this sense, the Bible is not just a comforting book that calms our fears and anxieties (although it does that too!), but the vision of God should make us uncomfortable, as we continually fall short of that vision due to our human sinfulness.

I take seriously the prophetic comment from Revelation 3:15–16: "I

know your works; you are neither cold nor hot. I wish you were either cold or hot. So, because you are lukewarm, and neither cold nor hot, I am about to spit you out of my mouth."

It is here that self-differentiated leaders have the courage to provoke, and even agitate to make a difference. However, as family systems theory acknowledges, it takes years of positive formation to create self-differentiated leaders, and there must be an atmosphere of encouragement in order for people to be formed in such a way.

## Individualized Consideration

The final descriptor of transformational leadership is called "individualized consideration," and the aim of this quality is the development of followers in coaching or mentoring them to reach individual fulfillment. It reinforces the larger goal of transforming people's lives. As spiritual leaders we want people to reach their own individual fulfillment, and our objective is the holistic health and well-being of the people we serve. Holistic fulfillment means physical, emotional, intellectual, and spiritual. Our central focus is the spiritual fulfillment of others, and we find our own individual fulfillment contingent on the other areas: physical health, emotional stability, and intellectual stimulation. As general practitioners in ministry, we often overlap into these other areas. For example, when it comes to physical health, we are in and out of hospitals with our parishioners on a regular basis, and often serve as a secondary source of medical interpretation for them. The medical lexicon is often technical and challenging, and we often interface directly with our parishioner's physician during our visitations. I remember in my ministry sometimes being the primary source of medical interpretation as my parishioner would be alone and not have family locally. We often learn so much about the illnesses that our laity go through that we become generically versed in medical conditions. I remember once visiting a patient I did not know, and we talked about his medical condition extensively. We were almost at the end of the visit, before I was going to ask to say a prayer for this person, when he said he had never met a medical doctor who talked so caringly about his condition with him. He thought I was one of his medical doctors!

We spiritual leaders are also on the front lines of people's emotional well-being. As pastoral counselors we care for their emotions as a byproduct of their souls. Often times, we are the first contact for parishioners going through emotional upheaval and turmoil. We must always be in touch with

our strengths and limitations here, and our best friend is often referrals to trained psychiatrists and therapists. However, ministry is about intimacy at its best, and we are inextricably bound with people's emotional lives.

Finally, spiritual leaders should be a factor in the intellectual lives of the people we serve. Our Western culture is dominated by data and information at every turn, and people are often overloaded. As spiritual leaders we are often looked to to sort through the tons of information and provide a sense of meaning to it all. Through sermons, Bible studies, and writing, people are asking for a sense of meaning. In this regard, we often serve as interpreters of reality for people, and with this role comes the great responsibility to provide a comprehensive and fair understanding of society and the world. We have to acknowledge our biases up front, and remain faithful to the spiritual core values of our faith, but we should strive for a sense of intellectual curiosity and openness. This task underscores our need to be lifelong learners, and for us to seek a multidisciplinary learning goal. We don't have to be experts in all fields, but we should read and study widely.

## Level 5 Leaders

One final research input to this discussion on spiritual leaders as transformational leaders: Jim Collins's work on "level 5 leaders" is helpful here. Collins does not classify level 5 leaders as transformational, but as one understands the characteristics of level 5 leaders it is hard to distinguish them from transformational leaders. The definition that Collins has for level 5 leaders builds on a series of numerical steps. Each level is iterative and lays the skill set foundation for the level that follows it.

The final level 5 is the "executive," who "builds enduring greatness through a paradoxical blend of personal humility and professional will."[30] Level 5 leaders tend to be not larger than life, charismatic figures, but self-effacing, even shy and reserved. They possess a ferocious commitment to the organization and also to the highest standards of leadership itself. Level 5 leaders have been promoted to the highest positions of their organizations, and in Collins' study represented the chief executive officer (CEO) of their respective companies.

One will notice that level 5 leaders have progressed through a series of leadership benchmarks and promotions. So instead of a pure leadership quality, level 5 leaders represent the empirical validation of Collins's research. However, the way level 5 leaders are described in the literature shows a very high correlation to transformational leaders. Collins did not wish to

call them transformational leaders, but they were in fact the same type of leader.

Here are some possible crossover characteristics of transformational leaders: level 5 leaders do not promote themselves personally but rather channel their ambitions into the organization itself. They are the epitome of servant leaders, who are willing to sacrifice their own gain for those whom they serve. Level 5 leaders also surround themselves with the best and the brightest, as they are not afraid of more gifted people shining more than themselves, but believe such people will enhance the objectives of the organization. Contrast this with egocentric leaders who surround themselves with "yes" people and pick weak successors who will make them look better after they have departed.

Finally, level 5 leaders do not deflect blame when things go wrong but take the responsibility for such blame onto themselves. The reverse of this scenario is also true, as level 5 leaders do not claim that they are the reason for any success but give credit to the workers when things go well.

In my first full-time appointment, I was a naïve twenty-six-year-old who had just graduated from seminary. The DS told me that he was considering me for three churches, and it really didn't matter much which one I was appointed to because they were all small and somewhat ready to die. I know he didn't mean it in this way, but that was like laying down the gauntlet to challenge me to succeed. Once appointed to one of those churches, I immediately clicked with the laity of the church, and together we entered into a transforming type of ministry. The church was averaging about thirty-five in worship, and after seven years we were over one hundred in worship, had programs galore, and had almost tripled our budget. More important, the church was teeming with life and vitality.

This example exposes a serious trap in ministry. That trap is to reinforce the "Great Man" theory of leadership. A fatal flaw would be to turn this into an ego boost and conclude that it was my leadership that enabled the church to grow. What God helped me to understand is that I wasn't transforming the ministry of the church—rather God's ministry was transforming me! It was God's transforming power through that little church where I was first appointed that molded, shaped, and sharpened me into a Christian minister. It was God's power to make all things new that enabled this flawed, sinful person to serve with the transforming power of Jesus Christ!

I have no false illusions of humbleness here. I was a young, fairly gifted, new minister who had a passion to succeed. Part of the success of the church

was due to a young and passion-filled leader. However, it was the unleashing of the laity that proved the prime reason that the church grew. Together we formed a strong ministry team, but in the end it was God who gave the growth. We were there at the right time together, but without the divine spark, we would not have grown like we did.

# Do This, Not That!

My prescriptive advice on transformational leadership is to always place a check on your personal ego. Very seldom in Christian ministry is this about you. Rather, it is about the kingdom of God and God's will. This works in two ways: one, do not be personally inflated with successes in the church because very seldom are we the sole reason for success. We are bit players in a divine drama where God is the one who brings about the growth or success. There are always others, circumstances, and just plain luck that contribute to any success. Second, don't ride yourself too hard for a failure, as even if you made the final decision to do something that did not work out, it is never all your fault. Again, circumstances, context, and lack of luck play a part in church failures. In my assessment, failures are great growth enhancers, as we learn more when we fail than when we succeed, and our leadership is truly tested in our ability to bounce back (resiliency) from any setback. It remains critical for us to practice what Jim Collins calls "autopsies without blame."[31] We can do this on a personal level or an organizational one, and probably should do both. However, the point is to learn from our failures, not to beat ourselves up over them.

# For Further Reading:
# Church Size Transitions

Gaede, Beth Ann, ed. *Size Transitions in Congregations*. Herndon, VA: Alban Institute, 2001.

Mann, Alice. *The Inbetween Church*. Herndon, VA: Alban Institute, 1998.

# For Further Reading:
# Emotional Intelligence

Boyatzis, Richard E., and Annie McKee. *Resonant Leadership: Renewing Yourself and Connecting with Others Through Mindfulness, Hope, and Compassion*. Boston: Harvard Business School Publishing, 2005.

Bradberry, Travis. *Emotional Intelligence 2.0*. San Diego: TalentSmart, 2009).

Ciarrochi, Joseph. *Emotional Intelligence in Everyday Life*. New York: Psychology Press, 2006.

Goleman, Daniel. *Emotional Intelligence*. New York: Bantam, 2010.

———. *Social Intelligence: The New Science of Human Relationships*. New York: Bantam, 2007.

# For Further Reading: Adaptive Leadership

Bassford, Virginia O. *Lord, I Love the Church and We Need Help*. Nashville: Abingdon Press, 2012.

Daloz Parks, S. *Leadership Can Be Taught: A Bold Approach for a Complex World*. Boston: Harvard Business School Publishing, 2005.

Heifetz, Ronald. *Leadership Without Easy Answers*. Boston: Harvard Business School Publishing, 1994.

Heifetz, Ronald, and Marty Linksky. *Leadership on the Line*. Boston: Harvard Business School Publishing, 2002.

Heifetz, Ronald, Grashow, Alexander and Marty Linsky. *The Practice of Adaptive Leadership*. Boston: Harvard Business School Publishing, 2009.

Williams, Dean. *Real Leadership*. San Francisco: Berrett-Koehler, 2009.

# For Further Reading: StrengthsFinder

Buckingham, Marcus, and Donald Clifton. *Now, Discover Your Strengths*. New York: Gallup Press, 2001.

Rath, Tom. *StrengthsFinder 2.0*. New York: Gallup Press, 2007.

Rath, Tom, and Barry Conchie. *Strengths Based Leadership*. New York: Gallup Press, 2008.

# Additional Qualities and Traits of Highly Effective Clergy

*Excellence is... **caring** more than others think is wise;*
*__risking__ more than others think is safe;*
*__dreaming__ more than others think is practical;*
*__expecting__ more than others think is possible.*
—Winston Churchill

Obviously, my big three in leadership development—a deep well of faith, emotional intelligence, and transformational leadership—are quite subjective in terms of prioritization. Check with anyone who thinks a lot about leadership, and they will probably have a different list. Debating one's priority list is rather fruitless, and I would be the first to acknowledge that there are dozens of other leadership qualities that can compete with these three. However, I believe that this is a good place to start.

I also want to share some additional qualities of highly effective UMC clergy that I found in my dissertation research. These are not meant to compete with my big three, and my advice is to first start learning, honing your skills, and coaching around the big three. For those high achievers who want additional input, these proposed qualities should round out my research.

# Collaborative Ministry and Empowering of the Laity

As already mentioned, transformational leadership is embodied in the collaborative leadership that sets people's strengths to work for the good of the whole. The most actionable way that highly effective pastors demonstrate transformational leadership is their empowerment of the laity of their churches. The key paradigm of this empowerment is the leader's ability to see the gifts in others, name and cultivate the gifts, and unleash these gifts and people into the ministry of the church and community. Empowerment of laity takes on the simple formula:

See—Name and Cultivate—Unleash

It is one thing to put this behavioral practice into place, but we would do well to remember the leadership qualities that maximize this process. As my research concludes, high emotional intelligence reinforces this empowerment paradigm. To see the gifts in others involves strong relational perceptions and the strength of a "relator." In the StrengthsFinder understanding, "relator" describes one's attitude toward relationships. The relator strength does not mean that you go out and make as many friends as you can, but rather you want to deepen the relationships that already exist or future relationships that matter to you. Relators crave intimacy and closeness, and seek out depth in their relationships. As clergy we meet many people on a regular basis, and we cannot develop deep relationships with everyone we meet. However, we can only see the gifts in others if we develop a deeper knowledge and understanding of others.

One of the highly effective pastors that I interviewed told me about the experience of a parishioner whom she did not know well. Serving a fairly large church this pastor had met the parishioner in worship, but he only came to worship and did not participate in leadership or other events. One day they talked more extensively after worship, and she found out that he was a major promoter of music concerts. This was around the time that Hurricane Katrina devastated the southern coast of the United States, and she had a vision of putting on a benefit concert to raise funds for the victims

of Katrina. He immediately identified with that cause, and volunteered to help out. What she didn't realize was how influential he was in the music industry. He got a major radio station to donate the tickets and publicity, got major musical performers to donate their time for the concert, and contacted sound and stage technicians to volunteer for the concert setup. Everyone in the church was astonished to see the commitment and expertise that this unknown parishioner brought to the church and this event. The concert was an unbelievable success, as people lined up hours before it began, and the line reached completely around the entire church campus. No one could remember the church being that packed with people. They raised thousands of dollars for Katrina, and the key was seeing the gifts of this one lone parishioner.

In this particular case, seeing the gifts of a major music promoter was a no-brainer, but often, it is the less dramatic gifts that we need to look for. So naming and cultivating gifts are critical in the empowerment process. Here, the qualities of being a good mentor are important to cite. Once we get to know people we can begin to identify their strengths and gifts, but for some people we have to do more by pointing out their gifts and cultivating them. Many people don't know their own strengths, and sometimes it takes another person to point them out. Clergy are in the unique role and position to be able to do this like no other profession. Learning how to successfully mentor is something of an art, but it is a skill set that can be learned and honed.

Mentoring involves us taking a personal interest in people, and more than that it means that we care enough about them to want to see them grow and improve. Encouragement, support, and cheerleading all have their place in mentoring. However, if we personally don't have an expertise in the gifts we are encouraging them to cultivate, then we have to put them in touch with those who have such demonstrated gifts. Networking is a fundamental skill here, as we mine our personal contacts to find teachers or knowledgeable people to connect them with.

The other side of networking is the ability to watch a person's strength with a task, function, or position that can best utilize the strength. Again, clergy are in the unique position of being able to do this in their role, as we see the many needs of the church and community, and should be on the constant lookout to match gifts with needs.

Another pastor that I interviewed talked about constantly seeing the gifts in others but said the real key is to match them with an unmet need in the church or community. He told me about his church's need to totally revamp their newsletter, and he happened to meet a relatively inactive daughter of one

Spiritual Kaizen

of the church's longtime members. She was a graphic artist by profession, and he told her about his vision for an improved newsletter. She got excited about the project and volunteered to help out. With her help, their newsletter was completely redone with a professional look, and they were able to acquire the new software and fonts to make their publications shine. However, the real plus of this story is that she became active in the church's ministry, not only with the newsletter but also in many areas of leadership.

If we work with the end in mind, which in this case is to unleash the gifts of people into the ministry of Jesus Christ, we follow a tried and true biblical model of leadership. We truly are "making disciples of Jesus Christ for the transformation of the world."

## Personal Humility and Passion for the Ministry

Another quality of the highly effective clergy whom I studied was a deep sense of personal humility. These clergy were at the top of their game, and commanded respect and admiration for their leadership, but they were genuinely humble about their accomplishments. Because of their faith groundings, they attributed any success to God and not themselves. In this respect, they exemplified Collins's level 5 leaders, people of "personal humility and professional will." As Collins states, "Level 5 leaders channel their ego needs away from themselves and into the larger goal of building a great company. It's not that level 5 leaders have no ego or self-interest. Indeed, they are incredibly ambitious—but their ambition is first and foremost for the institution, not themselves."[1]

The difference between highly effective clergy and secular level 5 leaders lies in the fact that clergy start with their deep well of faith as the basis of all their work. They realize that their gifts come from God, and their purpose is to use such gifts for the greater good of all. Because of their faith, they put their passion into love of God first, and then the church and community follow.

This passion for their work is shared by all of the highly effective clergy that I studied. Passion is a fuel, and they all demonstrated a high energy for their work in ministry. The genius of highly effective clergy is that they are able to focus and channel their energy into that which makes a difference. Energy alone is not enough—that can be random and scattered. Focus alone is not enough, as without energy it cannot be magnified. Both energy and focus together are necessary for success.

## The Focus-Energy Matrix

In an excellent article in the *Harvard Business Review,* "Beware the Busy Manager," Heike Bruch and Sumantra Ghoshal propose a "Focus-Energy matrix" that is enlightening. They see two characteristics in managers and leaders that will determine their work style and ultimate success: focus and energy. They define focus "as concentrated attention—the ability to zero in on a goal and see the task through to completion."[2] Energy is defined "as the vigor that is fueled by intense personal commitment. Energy is what pushes a manager to go the extra mile when tackling heavy workloads and meeting tight deadlines."[3] Their matrix includes four quadrants: low focus and energy, high focus and low energy, high energy and low focus, and high focus and energy. The following diagram will illustrate:

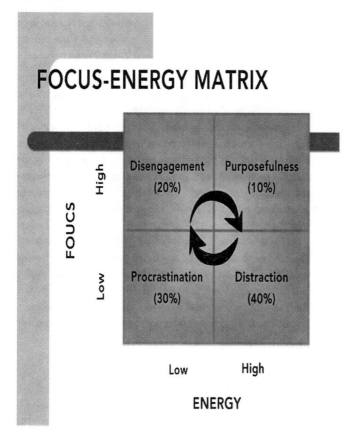

# FOCUS-ENERGY MATRIX

FOUCS

High

Low

| Disengagement (20%) | Purposefulness (10%) |
| Procrastination (30%) | Distraction (40%) |

Low        High

ENERGY

Low focus and low energy produces "procrastinators," and their research shows roughly 30 percent of managers fall into this quadrant. High focus and low energy produces the "disengaged," and 20 percent of managers fall into this quadrant. Regarding the largest group of managers, 40 percent fall into the high energy, low focus group, and they are called the "distracted." These are folks who feel compelled to do something and have the frenetic energy to be all over the map, but they do not have a specific objective that they can concentrate on. Often, they cause more problems than solutions. The final group possesses both high energy and high focus, and so they deserve the name the "purposeful." Only 10 percent of managers in their research are able to combine these two elements, and naturally, they get the most done and are the most effective leaders.

A major characteristic of the "purposeful" is how they approach their work. The purposeful generally work from the inside out: they figure out what they need to do and then work to manage the outside external environment. Their focus lies in setting their internal agenda and then managing their external environment where they put their energy into practice.

How do we get more clergy into the "purposeful" quadrant? I think performance coaching is probably the best alternative here. We can think of husbanding energy in the form of time and stress management, and learning to say "no." We know scientifically how to increase our energy levels through nutrition, exercise, and proper sleep and rest cycles. Focus can also be learned and developed. In my martial arts training, focus is a key element. The most popular form of focus is in the breaking of boards or bricks. In most martial arts, this is not an integral part of the art, but rather a showy part of demonstrations and public relations. However, the key to breaking a board or brick is in the concentrated focus that you bring to bear through the object which you wish to break. You focus all of your energy through the point of the object. There needs to be a solitary concentration through the object, and we call this "focusing through the break." I can usually teach almost anyone to break through a single wood board, and the same powers of focus can also be taught and coached with our clergy. It is a process of continually reminding them to concentrate on those objectives that will help them reach the church's goals.

# Mentors of Highly Effective Clergy

Before entering into the conclusions about mentoring, it might be important to point out the differences between mentoring and coaching.

Mentoring usually involves a more personal advocacy between individuals. It is akin to the more senior professional taking a younger and less experienced person under her or his wing. Mentors often act as guides that navigate the mentored individual through the complexities of a system or profession. Mentoring usually involves teaching and the imparting of wisdom.

On the other hand, coaching tends to be a more objective relationship that seeks to improve the performance, behaviors, and effectiveness of the one being coached. It usually tends to focus on results, with the desired hope to improve or grow the coached individual. The International Coach Federation (ICF) defines coaching as "partnering with clients in a thought-provoking and creative process that inspires them to maximize their personal and professional potential."[4]

There are many forms of coaching, and it tends to be situational or contextual in nature. There are executive, performance, and life coaches, and specific coaches for new church/congregational development pastors, turnaround pastors, and so on.

In making the case for mentors, all of the highly effective clergy that I studied had mentors and role models in their own ministry. Moreover, such mentors cut across the entire spectrum of these pastors' careers—starting when they were young or began thinking about ordained ministry, throughout their seminary education and early training, extending throughout their own pastoral ministry, and even when some of them are at the top of their careers, they still are influenced by mentors.

One of the key areas of learning from a mentor had to do with how one's mentor facilitated the process of self-discovery. In other words, mentors enabled these highly effective pastors to discover things about themselves that they had never realized or thought about before.

One senior pastor describes how a mentor pushed her into leadership. She was a college student at a large church, and they regularly brought all the youth groups together for music. Her mentor knew that she played guitar and said: "Oh, I'd like you to lead the music." She recalls that it really didn't go very well, and she was feeling bad about the whole experience. Her mentor addressed the situation in this way:

> He came up to me and he goes, "Sharon: that was a great beginning...that's just great, now let me suggest that next week when you do this..." And I thought, "Are you kidding—I'm never going to do this again in my life," and he didn't even

pause, "Next week when you do this, let me suggest that you keep a steady tempo when you do the song." He didn't even give me a chance to protest, or grovel to say how badly I felt, or I can't do this....Just moved it on. It was like he really believed in himself, believed in God, believed in me, threw me out there, but he was there with me.[5]

Not all of the mentors for highly effective pastors were clergy. In two instances, lay people and young adults (reverse mentors) were mentioned as mentors.

The effect of mentors clustered around some key principles:

- Role models and mentors were helpful in the process of self-discovery and self-analysis.

- Role models and mentors impacted the identity and current practices of highly effective clergy.

- Role models and mentors had an impact on the call and formation of these highly effective clergy in their vocation.

- Role models and mentors affected basic skill sets for these interviewed pastors, such as preaching, visioning, inspiration, leadership, and relational skills.

- The lack of female senior ministers as role models and mentors prompted the realization that women clergy face definite attitudes of sexism in their work as pastors in the church. These highly effective women clergy have learned to cope and deal with sexism, and ultimately to overcome its barriers, but the pain of dealing with sexism is real and harmful.

In addressing this last observation, all of the highly effective women clergy I interviewed gave personal testimony to the reality of sexism in their ministry. To underscore this point, a quick check with one of the chief researchers of The United Methodist Church pointed out that of the 730 local churches with an attendance of over five hundred in worship, he could identify only thirty women as senior or lead pastors (4 percent).[6]

The fact that the women pastors I interviewed had become district superintendents and lead pastors of large churches attests to the quality of their leadership. However, it did not diminish the reality of sexism in the church and their personal ministries.

# Lack of Formal Coaches of Highly Effective Clergy

An interesting note is that none of the highly effective clergy that I interviewed had formal coaches they used or met with regularly. This was an unexpected result in my research, as all of these highly effective clergy were lifelong learners, and were exposed to many pastoral resources.

In reflecting on possible reasons why there was little history of working with a coach by these pastors, one might suggest that the paradigm of coaching is still relatively new for the corporate world, and the religious community has not caught up yet. One might pair this with the fact that this is not a model that the religious community has developed in the past, hence the lack of a coaching paradigm in the church. These highly effective pastors have also been successful, and there hasn't been the great need for them to seek out a coach to help them.

This last point underscores the words of a very prominent coach who once remarked: "60 percent of clergy I cannot help with coaching; 30 percent I can help by improving their behavior and moving them to better results; and the last 10 percent are so good they don't need coaching, and they will get results without my help."[7] Currently, there is much more emphasis in The United Methodist Church placed upon engaging and using coaches for clergy and churches. Many annual conferences, cabinets, and staff people are providing regular coaching in many different forms: new church pastor coaches, turnaround church coaches, new clergy coaches, and so on.

There are more and more clergy who are becoming certified coaches through the secular coaching systems, and a number of annual conference cabinets that are moving to this paradigm. Many cabinets are also seeing more and more requests by individual clergy and churches to engage a coach.

In the future, coaching may become an established paradigm for The United Methodist Church and other mainline denominations. However, it is also clear that many highly effective clergy did not engage official coaches, and have succeeded without the need for external coaching. This sobering fact should warn us that not everyone needs formal coaching, and may seek out informal coaching and mentoring relationships on their own. There is much to learn about the coaching paradigm and pastoral effectiveness before we can draw definitive conclusions.

# Highly Effective Clergy Excel in Communications

Another correlation is that highly effective clergy excel in communications, both oral and written. They represent some of the best preachers in their annual conferences, and they are able to inspire, challenge, and teach through the medium of preaching. They are also strong writers and again, they leverage their collaborative work with the congregation through their written communication skills.

We would do well to remember the correlation between effective communication and effectiveness in pastoral ministry. In the attractional church model, worship still remains as the central galvanizing event of the local church, and these highly effective pastors attract and compel their members through strong preaching and communication skills. As we move into a missional model, strong communications will continue to play a role in the success of engaging one's surrounding mission field.

# Beyond the Pastor's Control: The Local Church's Situation and Context

Beyond any pastor's control is the fact that the local church's situation and context does matter. The demographics of both the church and the surrounding community, the past history of the church, the strength or weakness of its past lay and clergy leadership, the amount of resources the church has—all add up to make a big difference in the present and future success or failure of the church. As Gladwell has pointed out, the social science research often proves that situation and context are more important than character and attributes when it comes to people's actual behavior.[8]

This is especially relevant when we consider the nature of "challenging assignments." Remember the findings of the Center of Creative Leadership: 70 percent of growth in individual leadership comes from a challenging work experience. What this usually means is positive: a higher-level position, more responsibilities, more supervision, and more challenging problems. We have already established the fact that our mainline churches do not have many of these higher-level positions, and our challenging assignments are often taking churches on the brink of their organizational death back to life and health. It is all well and good if I am motivated by

**100**

bringing something from the bottom back to health, but often the response is depression and deflation rather than an energizing challenge. Thus, clergy start with the mental model of a "downward spiral"[9] that Rosamund and Benjamin Zander reference when talking about the *Art of Possibility*. With each new discouraging fact about the church on the decline, the spiritual leader gets more and more depressed—the church has lost twenty active members in the last year due to death and moving away . . . we cannot afford to pay a part-time secretary anymore, so you will have to do all of your own clerical work . . . the heater died last week, and we don't have any funds to pay for repairs and so forth.

Here, the challenges mount in reverse, and with each new setback, a spiritual leader can get more and more demoralized. The Zander model of downward spiral thinking is illustrated here:

The mindset that the Zanders advocate for is that of "radiating possibilities."[10] Instead of downward spiral thinking, you take the reality of the given situation, and you look for all the possibilities that can emerge: worship attendance is down—what possibilities are there to attract or reach out to a new constituency in the surrounding neighborhood? The church can't afford a secretary—who in the congregation has the skills to volunteer for such help? Maybe a team can be assembled to print the worship bulletin, put the newsletter together, and write correspondence. The church cannot afford to fix the heater—why doesn't everyone bring their winter coats to worship as the church members experience what it means to be without heat, and provide an extra coat to give out to the homeless in the area? Meanwhile, the church can work on fundraising using the symbol of a thermometer to chart progress toward a sixty-eight-degree heating environment. Networking and social media are critical, as the church can expand its need for a new heater to the broader community, searching for a personal contact with a heating company who might take up the cause by providing a low-cost heater and installation. The radiating possibilities go on and on.

Here is the Zander model of radiating possibilities:

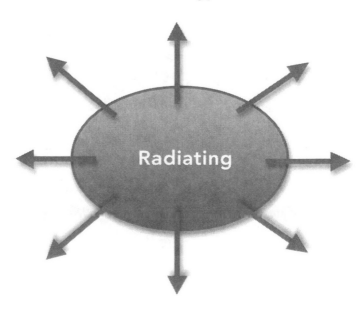

Before leaving this final issue of the church's history, context, and situation, one last story may be illustrative. Just as our genetic makeup determines much of our individual life, research now shows that the lifestyle we lead impacts our genetic markers, and can either positively or negatively affect them. In other words, if we practice an unhealthy habit like smoking, it will harm our genetic markers; whereas to practice a healthy habit like exercise will enhance those markers.

Much the same can be said of the current strength or weakness of the local church. To assess why a healthy church deteriorates, one can usually point to some key factors that contributed. It could be linked to unhealthy clergy or lay leadership, a major crisis of the church that was not handled well, or a major shift in the demographics of the surrounding neighborhood. The reverse is also true, for a successful and healthy church in the present; we can usually trace the health to a number of factors that positioned the church well.

One highly effective pastor who led a very large and vital congregation commented that one part of the church's current success can be traced directly to a major decision a former pastor made more than twenty years ago. At that time the church was on the edge of growth as the neighborhood demographic was growing. The church was faced with either building a new sanctuary, or making do with what they had and putting more resources into its childrens and youth ministry. The easier choice at the time would have been to raise major dollars to build a new sanctuary, but the pastor convinced the church to put that on hold, and put all of their resources into the growing demographic of children. They hired a professional assistant in children's and youth ministry, put in major resources and developed that ministry, and the children and youth came in abundance, and with them their parents. That one move made all the difference in the church's history from that point. The church grew and grew because of their excellent youth programs, and it is noted to this day as the church with an exceptional children's, youth, and young adult ministry. The current senior pastor remarked that if they had built a new sanctuary and not developed their children's ministry, they might not be a large and healthy church right now. If they had gone the other direction, after twenty years, they would have an aging sanctuary with half the people they now have. Their recent vacation Bible school maxed out on how many they can accommodate, and they had a large waiting list. In his estimation, this one decision was a watershed for the church, and set the stage for their later success. Incidentally, they did remodel and enlarge their sanctuary in the

process of their continued success, so they accomplished that goal while also growing.

The point is that major decisions can affect the church in dramatic ways, and good leadership tends to produce good decisions, whereas bad leadership may truly harm the church's future.

## Do This, Not That!

I have been using the concept of kaizen on an individual leadership level, but keep in mind that kaizen started at the organizational level, and it can be easily practiced at the local church level. One example comes from a retreat center that our annual conference used on a regular basis. Every time I returned to that retreat center some small new addition was noticeable. One time it was the addition of name holders on the sleeping room doors so people could put their business cards on the door to identify where they were located. Another time they had a seasonal prayer card placed on the desk in each room. Still another time there was the addition of a dessert cart. Each time I returned, there was a small yet noticeable improvement present. This is kaizen at its best! None of these changes was earth shaking or expensive, but they were clear improvements, and obvious. Needless to say, that retreat center continued to be profitable in the midst of a very tough market niche. Unfortunately, I can't think of a lot of our local churches that have adopted this same kaizen strategy, but when you think about it, it is so doable and simple.

## For Further Reading

Bolman, Lee, and Terrence Deal. *Leading with Soul.* San Francisco: Jossey-Bass, 2001.

Buckingham, Marcus, and Donald Clifton. *Now Discover Your Strengths.* New York: Free Press, 2001.

Friedman, Edwin H. *A Failure of Nerve: Leadership in the Age of the Quick Fix.* New York: Seabury Books, 2007.

Rath, Tom, and Barry Conchie. *Strength Based Leadership.* New York: Gallup Press, 2009.

(In both of the StrengthsFinder books above, there will be a code to allow you to take the StrengthsFinder assessment online—if you need to take the

assessment, be sure to get a new book and not a used one, in which the code will already have been used.)

Rath, Tom, and James Harter. *Wellbeing: The Five Essential Elements.* New York: Gallup Press, 2010.

Zander, Rosamund Stone, and Benjamin Zander. *The Art of Possibility.* Boston: Harvard Business School Press, 2000.

# The Critical Role of Church Culture, Systems, and Organizational Development

*Culture eats strategy for breakfast.*
—Peter Drucker

We have been progressing with the assumption that spiritual leaders can grow and develop on a lifelong basis (spiritual kaizen). In fact, unless we are committed to lifelong learning and development, we will cease to be effective in ministry. We may attempt to maintain our skills, but maintenance in this sense equates to decline. No one can stand still in the midst of the march of time. Either we continue to grow, or we decline. Staying relevant in ministry is the perfect example. If we don't continue to learn about pop culture, the latest in technology, or the most relevant trends in our world, that world will quickly pass us by.

One's personal commitment to growth in spiritual leadership is foundational. However, of equal importance are the church culture, the organization, and the systems that surround us. In fact, it is the classic chicken or egg quandary: does the culture create the spiritual leaders we have, or do those spiritual leaders create the culture? The correct answer is "yes." It is a "both/and" answer. We must pay attention to our own development and growth as spiritual leaders, but the culture and systems of the church have a profound impact on who we are as leaders.

Daniel Goleman, Richard Boyatzis, and Annie McKee have some key insights when it comes to the relationship between the organization's culture and the individual development of its leaders. They advocate that we start with a "process not a program." Here, the top leadership has to "get it," in that we begin by addressing the culture of the church. They recommend that we examine both the reality (what we actually do) and the ideal (where we want to go) in terms of leadership development. A good leader development system identifies who will be in the top leadership roles in the future, and grooms such people in the present.

But the most critical function is to design a process that continually builds leadership that gets results. That process includes three core elements:

• Help your leaders uncover their own dreams and personal ideals.

• Examine their strengths and their gaps.

• Use their daily work as a laboratory for learning.[1]

Before commenting on each one of these, it is important to note that in my study of highly effective pastors, one of the key learnings is that they possess both deep spiritual anchors and a strong grasp of leadership principles. They also practice these qualities on a regular basis, engaging in core spiritual disciplines (prayer, Bible study, devotional exercises, fasting, and so forth), and leadership practices (vision-casting, alignment, team building, etc.). Thus, highly effective pastors possess both spirituality and leadership knowledge. The common denominator between these two is the practice of the elements on a regular basis. The following diagram outlines this principle:

# REGULAR PRACTICES

I have often noticed that some clergy possess tremendous knowledge and command of spirituality, but lacking any leadership understanding, they do not know how to grow a church. The opposite is also observable: there are clergy who are up on the latest secular leadership principles, but lacking any depth spiritually, they too are unable to grow their assigned church. It seems that it takes both of these dimensions working together, but also put into regular practice, to make the difference in growth of a church. This underscores the author's third core process mentioned above: "Use their daily work as a laboratory for learning."

One thing we do not do very well in our seminary training is to teach prospective ministers how to learn on a daily basis. Seminary gives a tremendous amount of what to learn, and does this exceedingly well. A solid seminary education provides a general knowledge of biblical studies, theology, church history, ethics, world religions, pastoral care, education, church administration, and preaching and worship leadership. The closest other discipline to such comprehensive knowledge is medicine, where

all the medical specialties are covered leading up to a general practitioner. Most seminaries excel in providing the latest research and knowledge over these wide areas of thought, again leading to a general practitioner in ministry.

However, where the two disciplines part company in their pedagogy is in the area of supervised practice. Medical schools provide a strong experiential practice foundation, where students learn how to diagnose, examine, and treat actual physical aliments. Seminaries do not provide as comprehensive a program in supervised practice, usually requiring less than a full-time year in field education. Thus, seminary students must demonstrate a command of all of this knowledge, but do not have the same intensive supervised practice as medical students. Of course, the length of the two degree programs is a major factor here, with medical school requiring more than twice the amount of years in study as compared with seminary (four years of medical school, then four-plus years of residency compared to three years for a Master of Divinity).

Because the field education experience is so short, most recent graduates from seminary have not honed the practice of learning how to learn. It is here that the pioneering work of Chris Argyris and Donald Schon is helpful. When I was teaching in the seminary, I used their materials with the field education students, but the complexity of their thought and the intricacies of their methodology did not really translate well to the students. Much more work is needed in the translation of the material crossing over the disciplines of organizational development to that of the faith-based church. Work is also needed in bringing Argyris's lofty theoretical work to a practical model that the practitioner can engage in.

One example is Argyris's distinction between single- and double-loop learning. At its most elementary level, single-loop learning involves taking an action that produces results or consequences. How those results or consequences turn out largely determines what one's next action will be. The example often used for single-loop learning is the household thermostat. It is programmed for a certain temperature, and when it reaches that threshold, the furnace or air conditioner responds accordingly. Single-loop learning does not stop to ask why the temperature is set at that level; it is simply programmed and responds. The following diagram illustrates single loop learning:

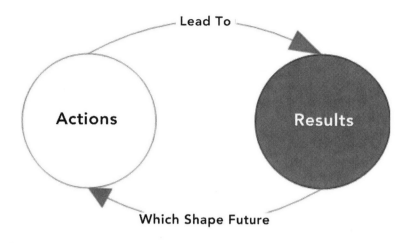

On the other hand, double-loop learning asks the additional question of "Why?" Another loop is added to the single circle above that raises the deeper questions that need to be asked in order to shape a more appropriate response or action. Argyris's theory gets more complex when he adds the human dimension of our propensity to create mental models, or beliefs of how reality is perceived. Each one of us holds onto a perceived understanding of "how things operate" in our own lives. In the case of the local church, a pastor will have his or her understanding of how things work and get done in that church culture. Double-loop learning adds the dimension that challenges us on whether our mental models are correct or effective in shaping our actions. The following diagram is illustrative of double-loop learning:

Double-loop learning adds the second reflection necessary to shape one's actions to get more effective results. Without the added reflection that asks why a previous action was successful or not, future actions lack the calibrated analysis of what works. Testing whether our beliefs or mental models are correct in every situation also helps calibrate the best response or action in the future.

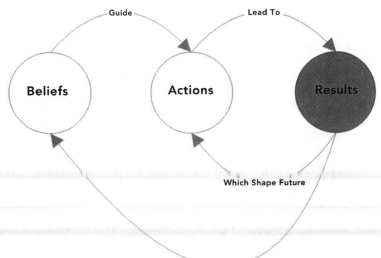

A specific example would be helpful: a young and gifted recent seminary graduate is assigned to her first full-time ministry appointment. It is to a small family-size church (an average of forty-two people in worship) that has been in existence for over 105 years. She is energetic and full of ministry ideas for vitality and growth. Her initial reception and acceptance is very positive and affirming. At her first administrative council meeting she shares many ideas, enables the group to organize around some of the ideas, and gives specific responsibilities. One of these is to start a new Bible study group around a relevant theme that seemed to resonate with the administrative council. When the time comes for the new Bible study group, only one person shows up, despite good and timely publicity. All of the other plans that were made at her first administrative council meeting also fail to materialize, and though she is disappointed, she rationalizes that the church is just not used to new activities and her energy. So, she tries again at the next council meeting to get things planned and organized. Once again, the council is affirming of these new plans, but once again none of the planning materializes despite her personal investment and planning.

Possessing a keen analytical mind, she decides to ask various members about this situation, and why nothing seems to happen from their planning. As she pieces together various vague responses, many of the answers

seem to lead to one of the old-time members who wields considerable influence over the entire church. She also checks with her mentors and teachers in the ministry, who point her to the church-size literature, and the fact that in family-size churches, the gatekeeper of the church controls much of what does and does not happen. She begins to understand that the pastor in family-size churches serves more in the capacity of chaplain, and in order for the church to grow to the next size, she must win over the trust of the members and serve as the center of a pastoral-size ministry. In reading this literature she begins to understand that the key lay leaders of the church exert the real power and decision making, and it takes almost ten years of continual service by the same pastor before they trust that the pastor is going to stay and allow that pastor more power. She researches the appointment history of the church and finds out that the church does not retain pastors for very long; the good ones move on to larger churches rather quickly, and the poor ones stay as long as they can until the church decides that they need a change. The more she learns about the culture of the church, the more she realizes that if the gatekeeper does not authorize a new direction or program for the church, it simply fails to happen or take root.

Through all of this learning, she begins to change her own mindset about the church and her own somewhat naïve belief that through her strong leadership alone, the church will change and begin to grow. So, she changes her actions. She immediately begins to work intently through the gatekeeper, winning him over, and getting his authorization for her program ideas. She purposely brings him into the leadership structure, and casts a new strong vision for the church and community. She also slows down her aggressive plans for the church, as she realizes that the most important thing is to gain the trust of the members, and this will take time and effort in showing them that she hopes to stay awhile and work for the best interest of the church. She is committed to stay at this church for as long as she can, and she shares this with members who think she will leave as soon as she gets a better offer. In her heart she wants to make a difference at this church in this community, and she is committed to staying. She reads and studies about church culture, and emulates the qualities of a pastoral-size church leader. By stepping back and reassessing her own beliefs and mental models, she adapts her actions, and the church begins to respond to her leadership.

This is a prime example of double-loop learning. Instead of the single loop of continuing to push the same actions over and over again, only to have them fail, falling into a state of frustration and anger, she steps away to add another loop of learning. Because ministry is so complex, these loops

never stop, and she must continually reflect on what works and doesn't work, adjust her mental models, and craft a new action strategy. She uses the church as her living laboratory, experimenting in real time, but always engaging in reflection about why something works or doesn't work. She also practices Jim Collins's suggestion of conducting autopsies without blame, taking apart and analyzing why something didn't work, but not personalizing it by blaming herself or anyone else. She also receives sound advice from her supervisors and mentors to take care of herself, work intentionally on her spiritual life, and practice life-giving self-care. She does this very well, and because of this the ministry remains joyful and challenging.

By her sixth year of such great spiritual leadership, the church has doubled in attendance, moved into the pastoral size, and looks toward a bright future.

## The Importance of Mental Models

As spiritual leaders one of the key areas of our growth is to be able to open up our mental models or mindsets in order to adapt to new situations and contexts. Roger Martin, dean at the Rotman School of Management at the University of Toronto, has done some major research on mental models and leadership. In his book *The Opposable Mind*, Martin argues that the most successful business leaders are those who exhibit "integrative thinking," or the ability to hold two opposite positions at the same time and not choose one over the other. They hold them in tension and come up with an original synthesized new version that is better than either alternative.

Martin defines our basic position as "stance," or "who you are in the world and what you are trying to accomplish."[2] We manifest our stance in the way we see the world, and how we see ourselves in that world. Integrative thinkers look at the world and themselves differently than most of us do. Here are the basic premises that integrative thinkers hold which are different from the majority:

STANCE ABOUT THE WORLD:

Existing models do not represent reality; they are our subjective constructions.

Opposing models are to be leveraged, not feared.

Existing models are not perfect; better models exist that are not yet seen.

STANCE ABOUT SELF:

I am capable of finding a better model.

I can wade into and get through the necessary complications.

I give myself the time to create a better model.[3]

Philosophically, the deconstructionists have long believed that human reality is not objective but is in fact a social construction of our own minds that is quite subjective in nature. Moreover, they believe that such a social construction cannot really be believed because it is based on the social limits of things like language and culture.

In other words, the mental models that we take for granted are not true in and of themselves but merely human constructs that people come to believe in. Integrative thinkers start with this very premise, and believe that the current models available are not the only ones, but rather just the ones that are currently popular. Optimistically, integrative thinkers always believe that there are better mental models and options yet to be devised, and they personally can come up with them. So, they have this uncanny ability to see two opposite positions or models, not accept either, and strategically position a third option that draws upon the strength of both opposites. Integrative thinkers are usually strategic and deep, and they are not afraid of messiness. In fact they thrive on the complicated and uncharted positions of the "not yet."

One of the basic tools to achieve the "not yet," Martin calls "generative reasoning." It is the form of reasoning that asks not "what is," but "what might be." In our Western educational system we use a different type of inquiry called "declarative reasoning." Because Western education is so dependent upon the Greek models of logic, both deductive and inductive, we operate with the either-or options of truth or falsity. This leads to a rigid form of reasoning that seeks the one right or true answer, and dismisses the unique shades of gray that are implicit in most reality. As Western-educated thinkers our mental models are based on what is currently true, real, and practically relevant, not on what is yet to be. However, true innovation and advancement comes not with declarative reasoning, but with generative reasoning. Integrative thinkers who practice generative reasoning are always searching for a new and better way to do something, or a creative solution that is different and better than what we currently have. Integrative thinkers go through a definite process of experimentation with new ways in order to get at the "not yet." Martin describes it this way:

Generative reasoning facilitates the trial and error that is integral to creative resolution. As integrative thinkers put their resolution through multiple prototypes and iterations, they use generative reasoning—to work back down from resolution to architecture to causality to salience. Large organizations may not recognize generative reasoning as a legitimate mode of inquiry, but they depend on it for lasting competitive advantage.[4]

One final point that Martin makes about true integrative thinkers: their goal is to acquire a mastery over the experiences that matter to them, but they also continually want to nurture their originality and innovation. These two goals are held in tension with each other.

In the church we often talk about mastering the practice of ministry. We point to highly successful pastors who are able to grow churches and create ministry vitality wherever they are appointed. Usually, with time, these pastors gain a mastery over their role and craft. Because they have practiced and improved their experiences in all forms of ministry, they have gained an intuitive skill set that has been honed by repetitive practice. However, it is not just practice that makes them masters. One can practice shooting a basketball a thousand times a day and over the course of years become an excellent shooter. But when you play in a game that really matters, it is not that you can shoot a basketball well, it is knowing when to shoot and when to pass the ball, seeing the flow of the game, and working with teammates collectively. In other words, it is putting all of the elements of playing the whole game together that produces mastery.

When I observe clergy who have mastered the art of ministry, it is not one element of their mastery that is impressive. It is not that they are merely exceptional preachers, teachers, counselors, administrators, or leaders, although they have mastered these specifics, but rather it is the combination of all of these gifts that results in their mastery.

Watch any pastor who has mastered the art of ministry and you will see a person who reads the situation and context, says the right and inspiring things, relates to people with the personal touch and care, and provides the kind of leadership that is needed at the right time. In other words, they put all of their experiences together to form their mastery of the craft. Simple repetition is not enough: one can practice the basics of ministry again and again, but rather it is the experimentation and learning of the right things to practice that make the lasting difference.

But as we have seen, it is not mastery alone that integrative thinkers rely on. Rather, it must be combined with the constant search for originality and innovation, which makes a true integrative thinker. This applies to spiritual leaders in the same way. The highly effective clergy who continue to grow and vitalize their churches combine mastery and originality as the foundation of their success. One without the other will not do. They are master practitioners who also continue to search for new and novel ways to carry out their ministry.

In my estimation, the mainline church has valued and honored mastery, but not originality and innovation. This latter area has been off our radar screen as a church. This is probably the reason for our huge decline, as we have been attempting to maintain our churches, not grow them. The typical life cycle of a church is often expressed in the following diagram:

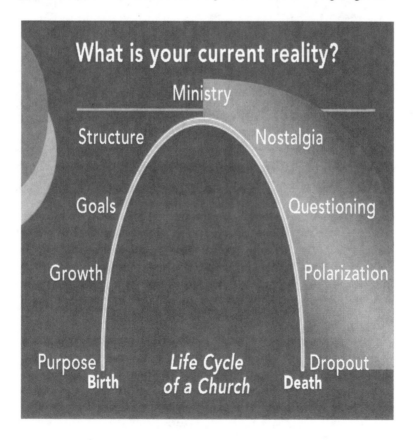

What is your current reality?

Ministry

Structure — Nostalgia

Goals — Questioning

Growth — Polarization

Purpose — Dropout

Birth — *Life Cycle of a Church* — Death

Notice the lack of innovation and originality concepts in this diagram. Now take a look at a typical secular business life cycle:

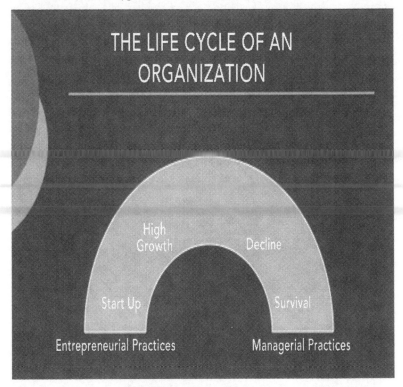

Innovation in the form of entrepreneurial practices is what fuels the growth of a secular business or corporation, and when managerial practices completely overtake the innovational practices, the company is in decline. You need at least a 50-50 ratio between these two practices to stay even, and most experts will tell you that for a company to stay competitive, you need a 70 percent entrepreneurial practice and 30 percent managerial practice ratio.

The closest concept we in the church have to entrepreneurial practices is evangelism or outreach, and our decline as the mainline church probably can be tied to the apathy with which we practice healthy evangelism and outreach. As established denominations, we have lost this outreach edge. Unless we can capture this sense of purpose to make disciples of Jesus Christ, we have little hope for true renewal.

Organizationally, how would such renewal work? When organizations plateau, some new innovation or outreach must spin the organization in a new direction. Before decline sets in, the organization is able to find a new innovation or originality to spin it forward again. The following diagram is illustrative of this notion:

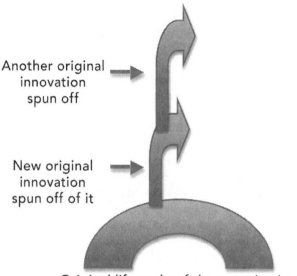

Another original
innovation
spun off

New original
innovation
spun off of it

Original life cycle of the organization

In this example, long before a church begins to decline, an original innovation for growth is conceived of and implemented, and that spins the church's growth forward until another novel growth idea emerges that takes it further. The cycle of new originality can continue to build, with each iteration replicating the healthy DNA of the original church, but building on a new platform.

An example of this growth pattern comes from the Philippines United Methodist Church. Part of their denominational DNA is that every church that reaches a certain size and health should then start another church in a new area. The key to their growth is that they don't wait until the founding church is a megachurch size. Rather, when the church reaches some stability, they automatically attempt to replicate themselves in another geographic area. This replicating model is part of their very identity and mission, so that originality and innovation is hardwired into the church's structure.

In the United States we need to come up with a similar model. But in order to do so, our mindset or mental model has to change from a consumerism–empire-building mentality to one of dynamic missions.

So, in terms of spiritual leadership, we must foster a balance goal of mastery and originality. As Martin suggests:

> The great ones utilize their experiences to build and deepen their mastery while maintaining and expressing their originality. Average leaders do one or the other. Some deepen their mastery over time but never learn to trust their ability to express originality. They keep the proverbial trains running but will never invent the future. "Watch out," warns Amy Edmondson of the Harvard Business School, "because our natural tendencies, the way we are hardwired, will lead us to favor mastery over originality, will lead us to keep going in the direction we are going and try to improve marginally around the edges on what we're already doing. In so doing, we utterly miss opportunities to make a big difference, something brand new and exciting."
>
> Others express their originality but do not develop their mastery. They are sought out as "idea people" but aren't trusted to run organizations of size and endurance because they can't or won't cultivate the multiple masteries that leadership of such entities demands.[5]

Martin concludes: "Mastery without originality becomes rote; originality without mastery is flaky if not entirely random."[6] He sees these two as interdependent, and they feed and enhance each other in ways that can never be predicted.

One final reflection point is to objectively see the predominant mental models of mainline clergy. Seminary education has a major influence on our clergy leadership, and we have already mentioned the generalist nature of seminary education. In this sense, clergy operate much as the medical profession's general practitioner: overseeing the overall health of the patient, but referring to the specialist when needed. This also reflects upon the tremendous role variation and volume of work in local church ministry. Merely keeping up with a busy church and community schedule is enough to burn out the most energetic pastor, so care has to be given to pace, volume of work, and role expectation. Those who do not have the energy can easily be buried in the rigors of a local church pastorate.

One current mental model that has tremendous influence through seminary education is the therapeutic model that is taught in pastoral care and counseling. The therapeutic model, with its emphasis on the self and subjective experience, presents a Western psychological grounding for most clergy. Think of the implications of that model: it is a one-to-one relationship that strives for a sense of healing of the individual. This is an appropriate context for a secular therapist or mental health professional, but it doesn't quite work in the postmodern church, where clergy do not have the luxury of spending so much in individual counseling. It somewhat fits the old paradigm of the attractional church model, where clergy reside inside the four walls of the church and parishioners come to the church for programs and counseling, but in the postmodern world of the missional church, where we have to engage people outside and in the surrounding community, the therapeutic model does not work. I would further push the point that clergy who operate out of the therapeutic model resist the postmodern missional turn, and want to preserve the dying paradigm of the attractional church.

Granted, family systems theory better incorporates the missional model, but the one-to-one healing foundation of the therapeutic model mitigates against the mindset of family systems theory. Had Edwin Friedman been able to complete his work on the application of family systems theory to organizational development before he died, I believe the field would have made a significant switch.

As I think of Jesus' healing examples, they also include one-to-one encounters, but they are mostly in the midst of large crowds, and are performed in a communal context, which speaks volumes for the postmodern missional model.

In my own local church ministry, I was under the influence of the therapeutic model, as I was taught by one of the giants of pastoral care and counseling, Howard Clinebell. Through the years, I came to realize how much time it took for individual counseling, and adopted the policy of doing only short-term one-to-one work (a limit of two to three sessions per person). One of my wake-up calls came in counseling with a couple who did not go to the local church that I was serving, but had heard that I helped another couple they knew. I had met with them a number of times to work on their marriage, when it hit me that they were basically receiving free counseling without any commitment to the church. There is absolutely nothing inherently wrong with that, but it did make me stop to realize how much time and energy I was putting in on this individualized counseling.

In the midst of trying to build the church and outreach to the community, I had to assess the value of my time in this context. Even with these free counseling sessions, they never did attend any of the church's worship services.

The other mental model that I think many of our clergy operate under is the "programmatic model," also taught in seminary and by the general church. In this model, we believe that if we can design and implement the right program for people, they will come and stay at the church. Such a programmatic mindset also influences how we deal with church problems. If we isolate a specific problem in the church, our natural tendency is to design a program to solve it. For example, the local church is having financial problems, so we believe that a stewardship program or special fundraising program will solve that particular problem.

Again, in my local church ministry, I was greatly swayed by this mindset, as I believed that the way to grow the church was to have tons of programs that attract different types of people. So I created all of these new programs, and it kept the church membership busy, and me overworked, but it did not dramatically increase outside attendance. For sure, new people did join the church, but I am not now convinced it was due to a dramatically increased program level.

The main point here is to recognize our own mental models. We need to do honest reflection on them, but also be open to new mental models that might tremendously influence our future ministry.

## Do This, Not That!

Because of our training and prevailing cultural ethos, it is easy to bypass or even dismiss the need for entrepreneurial innovation. In my estimation, to do so is tantamount to dying as a viable religion. One of the hallmarks of America has always been its innovative and entrepreneurial spirit, and U.S. religion reflects its own national values here.

As I have mentioned previously, to merely maintain the mainline church is surely to die an accelerated death. If we are to be viable for the future we are going to have to innovate and create new ways of being relevant. It is an adaptive challenge, and there are absolutely no blueprints or prescribed directions available. Each local church, regional ministry, and judicatory will have to reinvent itself and experiment wildly in order to find new ways to reach people.

Every spiritual leader must reach outside his or her comfort zone and

take on a more innovative and entrepreneurial mindset. No less than the very existence of the mainline Christian church is at stake!

## Don't Forget to Dream

Returning to our bright and gifted pastor who adapts successfully to her first church appointment, it would have been very easy for her to get discouraged and disillusioned. After all, seminary usually provides lofty visions and dreams of changing people's lives and the world around them. When the reality sets in that such changes will take time and will be resisted at many levels of the church, morale can become a major issue. Lacking the insight and skills to practice highly effective double-loop learning, many clergy simply give up their grand visions, and settle into lower expectations for truly transforming change. A creeping cynicism can set in, and without a string of successes coupled with strong self-care, many clergy get beaten down by the church. This is why Goleman's suggestion of "helping your leaders uncover their own dreams and personal ideals" is so important. How often do our judicatories provide the forum and expertise to recover our original hopes and dreams for the church when we started our ministry? This is not on the radar screen for most judicatories, and the highly effective clergy figure this out by themselves, and continue to thrive in the ministry, while the majority of clergy lose their original hopes and dreams, and suffer from low morale.

As a bishop I take this challenge very seriously. As of late, I have decided to work with small geographic clusters of clergy to address this issue of morale, and try to recover their sense of hopes and ideals. We meet in small covenant groups, share joys and sorrows, and then go through an exercise to remember our original dreams for ministry when we first started. We also think to the future, and cast a vision of what the church can be. I am struck by the energy that emerges when clergy get in touch with their hopes and dreams. I then ask them to lead another small group of their own with their church or other ministerial colleagues to engage in a similar exercise. I find these groups life-giving for many clergy, and I am sorry that I didn't start these types of groups much earlier in my supervised ministry career.

As to Goleman, Boyatzis, and McKee's third point—"examine the strengths and the gaps" of one's employees, and in the church's case, of the clergy—I find once again that morale drops when we only dwell on deficiencies and weaknesses. As mentioned previously, the Gallup Strengths Finder program believes that focusing on strengths rather than trying to

fix weaknesses is the key to long-term success. Their signature line here is "weakness fixing prevents failure. Strengths building leads to excellence."[7] By accentuating the natural strengths of individuals, one leverages what they can do best, and they remain engaged because they work out of what they do best and not what they are weak at. This does not mean that the StrengthsFinder philosophy is to ignore weaknesses or gaps. Rather, it is to manage them, but not to dwell on fixing them. The StrengthsFinder assessment provides a range of thirty-four signature strengths, and enables individuals to understand and work from their top five strengths.

So, the key here is educating our clergy to know their strengths and gaps in order to work on accentuating their strengths and managing their weaknesses. My long-term hope is that each minister in our entire annual conference will have a complete dossier of his or her strengths, skill sets, and spiritual gifts. All of this information will be electronically available, and each district superintendent will have the files of the clergy they supervise on an iPad or computer. Likewise, each local church will have a complete assessment of its ministry, neighborhood demographics, ministry strengths and gaps, and what it needs in the future to thrive. With such a database, it will be much easier to match strengths and skill sets to individual clergy and church needs. I even dream of a specialized computer software program that automatically matches clergy strengths with local church needs!

After establishing the groundwork of this leader development, Goleman, Boyatzis, and McKee then caution us with this admonition: "avoid the trap of providing another executive education class or program." I find this advice so important to heed. As Matures and Baby Boomers in ministry, our automatic default response to any problem or concern is to create a program to address it. This has been a part of our seminary training, and it harkens back to the way the church operated in the 1960–70s. It was a programmatic model of ministry that operated on the assumption that people would naturally affiliate with a Christian local church, and providing quality programs was the key to attract them to the church.

However, in the face of such dramatic society shifts, the program model does not work well. Whereas the church used to thrive on the "attractional" model where people sought out affiliation with the church, now people are just not interested in attending a church, regardless of how fantastic the church programs are. So, we find ourselves now in the mode of the "missional" model of going outside of the four walls of our churches and seeking out people where they naturally gather. This can run the gamut of bars and pubs to small monastic communities that people are interested in forming.

So for the most part we find the programmatic model a bankrupt tool in the missional outreach age. If we are to work on the leadership skills of our clergy and laity, we should avoid the trap of simply providing more training programs in order to "fix" our people. We have to look much deeper than this to work on and improve all of the leadership systems of our church. We have to also realize that trying to fix people is a very short-sighted approach to leadership.

In a fascinating doctoral dissertation, Marco Cavazzoni engaged in a social scientific study of the effectiveness of a major corporate executive leadership program of a major aerospace company. His conclusions included the fact that a well-designed executive leadership program does have short-term benefits to the leaders and organization, but unless there is follow-up training, the leadership outcomes are not effective. There is an initial honeymoon period where the trainees attempt to enact what they have learned, but without reinforcing follow-up, the vast majority of those who were put through the executive training go back to their standard leadership practices within a six-to-nine-month period. In other words, they do not change at all. He also suggests that a quantitative evaluative analysis is absolutely essential in determining the effectiveness of such leadership enhancing programs, and in the case of his company, a multi-million dollar executive education program was simply not working.[8]

Goleman, Boyatzis, and McKee follow up with a more helpful alternative, and that is to "develop a holistic leader system that permeates every layer of the organization." They believe that "true change only occurs through a multifaceted process that penetrates the three pivotal levels of the organization":

The individuals in the organization

The teams in which they work

The organization's culture[9]

For us in the church, our "individuals" are both our clergy and laity together.

Developing a program that focuses on "fixing" our clergy only is to miss the holistic nature of the church. First, it wrongly focuses blame on the clergy who need fixing. Second, it is the laity who hold the greatest potential for leadership and direction in our churches. We have consistently underutilized our laity in their secular expertise in the church. Under the guise of not wanting to burn them out, or have their work bleed over to

the church, we have robbed our laity of their natural strengths that can be leveraged for the good of all. We have every level of secular expertise in the laity of our churches. Marketing, personnel, strategic planning, finance, construction, real estate—you name it in terms of areas that clergy are not trained in or do not excel at, and our laity possess it. Most laity can do these types of skills in their sleep, and giving the church some of their natural abilities and skill sets is often a joy rather than a burden. Again, this is a matter of leveraging the strengths of people rather than forcing them to do something that they are not good at or do not enjoy doing. In general, the church does not do a very good job in volunteer placement. Why have a chief financial officer of a large company serve as a worship greeter? Why not put her in a major finance position where her expertise can make a huge difference in the church and community? Why have an electrical engineer chair your education department when that person could coordinate your short-term missions rebuilding programs and use his or her expertise in the rebuilding projects? The list goes on and on, and the point is unleashing our laity to be the transformational presence in our churches and communities.

Of course, there are laity who wish to get away from their jobs and volunteer to do something quite different at the church. A healthy respect for the passion of individuals is key in this strategy. The point is for the church to know and utilize the passions of its members, and this requires the church to do a better job in the field of human relations.

The most effective training is when the pastor(s) and a group of leaders of the church experience the training together. They learn, are motivated, and are aligned to a common purpose together. One can put on the best training events in the world, but if only isolated individuals go through the training, the information remains in isolation. The rest of the church has not experienced the learning, excitement, and effectiveness of that training. Too often isolated individuals are set up to fail when they experience a new way of looking at and doing church by themselves. Shared community is the key, and unless you can get a minimum of 20 to 30 percent of your congregation behind a new way of doing things, most likely it will die due to isolation.

Goleman, Boyatzis, and McKee's second layer of penetration involves the teams in which people work. There is a natural affinity that takes place with teams. Not only is there a common identity that forms with teams, they can be a collective source of implementation and change. Some churches are getting great results from short-term missionary teams that continue to meet after the missions project is over as a small discipling group. They get to know and enjoy each other while working together, and it is natural to

keep them together in community. Once you establish a purposeful process with such small groups, they can be a healthy source of discipling in the church. Many churches use missions projects as the central creator of new small groups, and over time, with a well-defined process of discipleship, the small groups continue on and serve in the assimilation of new members into the life of the church.

The process of creating great teams in the church can be limitless. At the heart of what the church does well is the formation of study teams, work teams, administrative teams, and so on. What we have to learn how to do better is the creation of great teams. Here, great teams must have a central and compelling purpose, great leadership, the development of an individual's strengths, and the prospect of challenging (but not too challenging) growth and learning. The values of trust, collegiality, affinity, and joy must be present in abundance.

Goleman, Boyatzis, and McKee's final point of penetration is the most important: the organization's culture. The reason why so many corporate change programs fail is the fact that the culture of the organization fails to change. Professor and consultant Edgar Schein provides the most depth in understanding and impacting the culture of the organization. Schein provides a comprehensive outline of organizational culture:

Artifacts (visible organizational structures and processes)

Espoused beliefs and values (strategies, goals, and philosophies)

Basic underlying assumptions (unconscious, taken-for-granted beliefs, perceptions, thoughts, and feelings).[10]

Under such broad categories, almost any element of culture can be identified and located. It is interesting to note that Schein describes the three points above as "levels," asserting that there exists a hierarchy of depth to the three dimensions of culture. However, it is far from a simple hierarchy, as he comments that the " 'climate' of the group is an artifact of the deeper cultural levels, as is the visible behavior of its members."[11]

Even with the complexity of Schein's tri-level cultural paradigm, there appear to be some deep-seated cultural values that lie at the very heart of any given organization. This is Schein's third level of basic underlying assumptions. Again to use a metaphor, if we peel away the husks of the organization to uncover the kernels of essence of the organization, we may find its central purpose and meaning.

Another famous researcher and consultant, Geert Hofstede, has a similar paradigm in his discussion of cultural elements. His metaphor is peeling "successive skins of an onion, from shallow superficial symbols to deeper rituals." He asserts that symbols, heroes, and rituals can be classified under the term "'practices', because they are visible to an observer although their cultural meaning lies in the way they are perceived by insiders."[12]

However, the core of culture is formed in the "values." Schein defines values "in the sense of broad, nonspecific feelings of good and evil, beautiful and ugly, normal and abnormal, rational and irrational—feelings that are often unconscious and rarely discussable, that cannot be observed as such but are manifested in alternatives of behavior."[13]

Schein believes that change must happen at all three levels to be effective. However, the "basic underlying assumptions" level is the most difficult to penetrate and to quantify. Think for a moment as if you are a new employee of a company, and you are trying to understand the company's culture. You can see artifacts and espoused beliefs in what the company displays and through presentations. However, it will take time and effort for you to uncover the "unconscious, taken-for-granted beliefs, perceptions, thoughts, and feelings" of the company. These are usually so ingrained in the ethos of the workers that no one talks about them, and employees just live the values of them as they survive or thrive in the company itself.

In order for true change to take place, all of Schein's levels must be penetrated with a new ethos. Anything less than changing the fabric of the culture itself will end in failure.

What any change leader will find helpful is Schein's model of primary and secondary mechanisms that a leader can use to induce cultural change:

**Primary Embedding Mechanisms**

- What leaders pay attention to, measure, and control on a regular basis

- How leaders react to critical incidents and organizational crises

- How leaders allocate resources

- Deliberate role modeling, teaching, and coaching

- How leaders allocate rewards and status

- How leaders recruit, select, promote, and excommunicate

**Secondary Articulation and Reinforcement Mechanisms**

- Organizational design and structure

- Organizational systems and procedures

- Rites and rituals of the organization

- Design of physical space, façades, and buildings

- Stories about important events and people

- Formal statements of organizational philosophy, creeds, and charters[14]

For example, "What leaders pay attention to, measure, and control on a regular basis," may seem obvious, but the subtleties may escape us. It is very clear that people pay attention to that which the leader deems important. For the mainline church, the problem has been the question of focus or prioritization. In most mainline denominations, everything is important and critical. In The United Methodist Church, we possess a very big tent in terms of continuums and polarities. As a very large denomination we always skirt a delicate balance between diverse constituencies. We believe in evangelism and peace and justice; we believe in individual rights and communal values...we believe in personal piety and social holiness. Our problem has been that everything is of equal importance, and the saturation point of our followers in terms of the sheer volume of what we deem important is overtaxed. If everything is important, then nothing ends up being important, because people have no way to prioritize an ever expanding list.

As leaders we must prioritize very carefully what we deem to be the

most important issues, pay keen attention to them, and demonstrate how we are to measure and control such priorities. For me, the central mission and purpose of The United Methodist Church must be messaged in a consistent and repetitive fashion. As mentioned previously, our mission is "to make disciples of Jesus Christ for the transformation of the world." That mission must be central, and all things should flow from that purpose. In the annual conference that I serve, that remains our central mission, and all the important priorities serve that mission. How we measure that mission is embodied in the metrics we pose to each local church:

**10 percent** net increase in worship attendance.

**5 percent** net increase in professions of faith.

**2** new outreach or evangelism programs to the neighborhood or community.

**2** new small groups that will foster discipleship for the life of the church.

**100 percent** payment of apportionments.

I am also counting on each local church to make sure it has two key systems:

A **discipling system** that brings people into a deeper relationship with Jesus Christ.

An **outreach system** that reaches out into the mission field.

In order to emphasize our shift to the mission field, our Pacific Northwest Annual Conference is using the tagline: "Every local church a mission center, and every United Methodist member a witness."

What we are finding is that people are getting the central message of mission-field engagement, but are lacking the skill sets to actually do it. We hope to follow up with extensive training and development of new skills to engage the community in a whole new way.

As a bishop and cabinet of district superintendents, the one thing that is under our control is the appointment of clergy. If we are true to our mission statement of making disciples of Jesus Christ for the transformation of the world, then all the appointments we make must flow from that central purpose. So, we have a value system that guides our appointment process, and in strict priority we attempt to place clergy by considering in descending order:

God

The Kingdom of God as expressed in the local mission field

The local churches

The clergy

The annual conference

The bishop and cabinet

## Do This, Not That!

As spiritual leaders we must not follow the denomination's inability to prioritize and focus. Remember the "focus-energy" matrix by Bruch and Ghoshal: truly effective managers combine both energy and focus in their work. One without the other leads to less effectiveness in leadership. It is critical for us to focus our energy on that which makes a difference in our ministry and not be distracted by the myriad of duties and roles that we have traditionally assumed. This means that we set priorities on a regular basis, and we work on the most important actions first. I try to set priorities daily, weekly, monthly, quarterly, and yearly. This involves the discipline to set aside some intentional planning time to work on a list of priorities using this time sequence. I then refer to these lists on a regular basis, and they form the foundation upon which I make choices about how to give my energy and attention.

## How Leaders Recruit, Select, Promote, and Excommunicate

One of Schein's key areas of focus is worth considering: "How leaders recruit, select, promote and excommunicate." This is very close to Jim Collins's "people first" principle of "Getting the right people on the bus, and the right people in the right seats."[15]

In The United Methodist Church, bishops do not decide on the ordination of the clergy who serve in local churches. By our polity that is the role of the Board of Ordained Ministry. The United Methodist Church *Book of Discipline* has put some strong firewalls between the cabinet and the Board of Ordained Ministry as a form of checks and balances. The Board of Ordained Ministry selects in the form of commissioning and ordination of ministerial candidates. The cabinet then takes such selections and appoints these spiritual leaders to specific local churches. For maximum

diversity, the cabinet cannot ordain those whom they want to appoint, and vice versa, the Board of Ordained Ministry cannot place those whom they select. However, the downside of our system is the fact that when there is no intentional communications between the two groups it is akin to having your company's personnel department not talking with your management department in deploying the workers. How would the personnel department know what management needs in terms of numbers and skill sets?

Therefore, it is critical that the bishop and cabinet have a healthy and communicative relationship with the Board of Ordained Ministry. As a former chairperson of the Board of Ordained Ministry, I have always had an affinity and love for that work. So, now that I have become a bishop, one of my primary cooperative relationships is with the Board of Ordained Ministry. If communication and cooperation breaks down between these two key systems, the whole selection and deployment process suffers.

The issue of recruitment remains our UMC's Achilles heel, in that no one has primary responsibility for recruitment in practice. Disciplinarily, recruitment is the responsibility of many entities: the local church, the Staff-Parish Relations Committee (personnel committee), the local church clergy, the District Committee on Ordained Ministry, the Board of Ordained Ministry (ordaining bodies), and the bishop and cabinet. However, because every one of these groups is overtaxed, recruitment usually gets put on the back burner. So, we end up with a "passive recruitment system," in the form of processing whoever shows up with an interest in ordained ministry. Instead of recruiting the best and brightest of our young people and laity, we end up settling for almost anyone who has a personal calling into ministry. We also miss all of those gifted people who never darken our institutional doors as members or attendees. If we are truly serious about leadership in The United Methodist Church, we will have to do intentional recruiting of the top students and laity both inside and outside of our churches.

In terms of the concept of "promotion" we have to recognize the huge paradigm shift that has taken place in our churches through the years. In the 1960–70s when the demographic of clergy was younger, newly graduated clergy would be deployed in smaller churches, or in associate positions under a senior pastor, and there was an expectation that if you did well, you would climb the ladder of church size, moving to larger and more influential churches as the years went by. Middle judicatory jobs such as district superintendent would also be the expectation for those who were successful in climbing the ministry career ladder.

However, everything has changed for the mainline Protestant churches through the years. There are fewer large and medium-size churches with vital ministries taking place. As church attendance has shrunk, many churches are on the edge of survival in terms of finances, attendance, and vitality. As mentioned previously, the percentage of "turnaround" church situations has dramatically increased, and a whole new set of skills is needed to provide pastoral leadership. As local budgets have shrunk, associate minister positions that used to be a training ground for young clergy have dried up, and with them, the chance to apprentice under a seasoned and experienced senior pastor. The other implication of less financial resources is that full-time secretaries and administrators are now a luxury that many churches cannot afford. So, one might find medium-sized churches with two hundred or more in worship without a full-time secretary. In many ways, there are fewer and fewer promotions in terms of moving to a larger church setting. Now lateral and even downward moves in church size are more the norm.

The notion of promotion is further complicated by the tendency of clergy to get locked into the pastoral-size mentality. We have addressed this throughout the body of this book, but many clergy try to do it all, fail to empower their laity, and stifle growth past the pastoral-size church. We have to find a way to break this habit of staying in the pastoral-size mentality, and enable our clergy to grow their churches to the next level (the program size), or when they are appointed to the program-size church enable them to remake their ministry so as not to reverse the growth back to the pastoral size. I firmly believe that this problem can be addressed through training, development, and coaching. If clergy are willing to grow and learn, they can move out of the pastoral size mentality, and remake themselves to the next growth level. However, I underscore the need to be open to growing and learning. Many clergy say that they are open, but in fact are not willing to change and adapt.

This brings us headlong into Schein's final suggestion of how leaders excommunicate, or get the wrong people off the bus. I do not believe that we have a large number of our clergy who need to leave ordained ministry, but there are those who are so toxic that we must exit them from ministry. There are a small minority of pastors who have severe personality disorders that actually drive people away rather than bring people to them and the church. Because we try to model the grace of God in Jesus Christ, we are slow to move them out of ministry, despite the need to do so, and waiting to see if they improve harms more people and themselves. It is more humane to get them out of ministry early. Jesus was equally clear about slow and hesitant followers (Matt. 8:19ff; Luke 9:57ff).

**133**

The second group of clergy who need to find new professions are those who are unwilling or unable to learn and change. If a minister is unteachable in new knowledge, skills, or learning from experiences, then there is little prospect of him or her doing well in the ministry. The pace of change has been so rapid in our society and world that spiritual leaders have to learn and grow on a continual basis. Lifelong learning is not a mere cliché, but rather the absolute norm if we are to adapt and survive in an ever-changing context. Adaptive leadership is all about the framing of new questions that will enable the church to move into the future. Adaptive leadership in the church means a constant set of new experiments to see what works and what doesn't. Literally, it is how we evolve in the church to be relevant. Those clergy who cannot or will not adapt will have to be moved out of ministry. Hopefully, they will see that they are mismatched in pastoral ministry and exit on their own accord, but if they do not see that, the church will need the courage to move them out of ministry.

Much of what was mentioned above pertains to the laity of the church also. There are laity who drive people away, and refuse to adapt and learn. We have whole local churches that are so hard on appointed clergy they have a history of harming their clergy. In these cases, the leadership of the denomination must have the courage not to send new ministers until the church is willing to deal with its dysfunction.

The best analogy here is that of the human body as a system. Healthy cells create health for the whole body. Harmful cells in the form of viruses and infections are attacked by the natural defenses of the body itself. Toxic or harmful members of the body, be they clergy or laity, must be addressed by the health of the system itself. If 99 percent of one's congregation is healthy, it is not right to allow 1 percent of that body to destroy the whole. The healthy 99 percent needs to address the toxicity of the few, and take proactive actions to preserve the health of the whole body.

I realize that as the church of Jesus Christ we must always err on the side of grace. However, protection of the innocent and good must also be a core value, and when a toxic person threatens the health and welfare of the whole, that person must be dealt with directly and removed if necessary.

In summary, change of culture is a huge and complicated undertaking. It is beyond the scope of this book to address the specifics, but please check the bibliography for reading suggestions on the change literature.

# For Further Reading: Organizational Development and Change

Bridges, William. *Managing Transitions: Making the Most of Change*. Philadelphia: De Capo Press, 2009.

Cohen, Dan. *The Heart of Change Field Guide*. Boston: Harvard Business School Publishing, 2005.

Holman, Peggy, Tom Devane, and Steven Cady. *The Change Handbook*, 2nd ed. San Francisco: Berrett-Koehler, 2007.

Quinn, Robert. *Deep Change: Discovering the Leader Within*. San Francisco: Jossey-Bass, 2010.

Rendle, Gil. *Journey in the Wilderness: New Life for Mainline Churches*. Nashville: Abingdon Press, 2010.

Schein, Edgar. *Organizational Culture and Leadership*. San Francisco: Jossey-Bass, 2002.

# CONCLUSION

A bonus chapter and appendix to this book include a process for the reader to organize all of the information and design a customized personal leadership plan. The appendix provides an actual template in doing this important work. To access these materials, go to http://abingdonpress.com/hagiya.

I hope you apply this book and create your own personal leadership plan. This final step is the natural conclusion to the central thesis of this book: leadership is not innate; rather we learn and grow into leadership, and we can do this in a slow, steady, but progressive fashion (spiritual kaizen).

I also pray that you will not give up on the Christian church. These are hard times for the mainline denominations. We face unparalleled challenges in a changing ethos of Western society that is leading to the decline in our numbers and influence. I firmly believe that the Church of Jesus Christ will never end. Individual denominations will wax and wane, but Christianity will find a way to reinvent itself to captivate new generations of believers. The renewal of the church is not solely in our human hands; God will provide the ways and means for it to happen. Certainly, if we are not open to the winds of the Spirit, we will hasten our own demise as a church. This is where leadership makes the difference—leadership that continues to experiment, adapt, and change. Ultimately, God will provide the way for us to succeed, and leadership will make the difference by following that lead.

My prayers go with you in your spiritual leadership.

# NOTES

## Chapter One: Spiritual Leadership 101

1. Kenneth D. Strange, "Examining Effective Technology Project Leadership Traits and Behaviors," *Computers in Human Behavior* 23 (004), 431.

2. Peter G. Northouse, *Leadership: Theory and Practice*, 4th ed. (Thousand Oaks, CA: Sage, 2005), 19–21.

3. Bruce J. Malina and Richard L. Rohrbaugh, *Social-Science Commentary on the Gospel of John* (Minneapolis: Fortress, 1998), 126.

4. Daniel Goleman, "Leadership That Gets Results," *Harvard Business Review* 78, no. 2 (2000): 78–90.

5. Ibid., 80.

6. Ronald Heifetz and Marty Linsky, *Leadership on the Line* (Cambridge, MA: Harvard University Press, 2002), 20.

7. Juan Luis Segundo, *The Liberation of Theology* (Maryknoll, NY: Orbis, 1976), 157–60.

8. Linda Moorman, personal communications, November 8–9, 2011.

9. Ibid.

10. Ibid.

11. Center of Creative Leadership Leading Effectively e-Newsletter, November 2011, "The 70-20-10 Rule," 1.

12. Ibid., 2.

13. Richard DeShon and Abigail Quinn, "Job Analysis Generalizability Study for the Position of United Methodist Local Pastor," unpublished paper, Michigan State University, 2007, 20.

# Chapter Two: Our Present Reality

1. Richard Southern and Robert Norton, *Cracking Your Congregation's Code* (San Francisco, CA: Jossey-Bass, 2001), 54.

2. The Pew Forum on Religion and Public Life: *US Religious Landscape Survey,* 2008.

3. The Pew Forum on Religious and Public Life: *"Nones on the Rise,"* Oct. 9, 2012.

4. Tom Butcher, personal communication, September 29, 2008.

5. Ibid.

6. Campbell and Company: "Generational Difference in Charitable Giving and in Motivation for Giving," May 8, 2008.

7. William G. Enright, personal communication, November 18, 2011.

# Chapter Three: The Big Three of Spiritual Leadership

1. John Cobb, personal communication, 1990.

2. Gustavo Gutiérrez, *We Drink from Our Own Wells* (Maryknoll, NY: Orbis, 1974), 1.

3. John Mayer, Peter Salovey, and David Caruso, "Models of Emotional Intelligence," in R. J. Sternberg, ed., *Handbook of Human Intelligence,* 2nd ed. (New York: Cambridge University Press, 2000), 396.

4. Daniel Goleman, Richard Boyatzis, and Annie McKee, *Primal Leadership: Learning to Lead with Emotional Intelligence* (Cambridge, MA: Harvard Business School Press, 2002), 39.

5. Jim Collins and Morton Hansen, *Great by Choice* (New York: HarperCollins, 2011), 78.

6. Ibid., 78–79.

7. Ibid., 94.

8. Ibid., 83.

9. Derek Nakano, personal communication, August 5, 2010.

10. "Entrepreneur," in *Business Dictionary Online,* http://www.businessdictionary.com/definition/entrepreneur.html, retrieved February 2, 2011.

11. Ibid.

12. Lee Hayward, personal communication, February 26, 2012.

13. Robert T. Wilson, "Servant Leadership," *Physician Executive* 24 (1998): 6–13.

14. Robert Greenleaf, *The Servant as Religious Leader* (Peterborough, NH: Windy Row Press, 1982), 91.

15. *The Book of Discipline of the United Methodist Church,* 2004, 92–93.

16. Ibid., 93.

17. Phil Amerson, personal communication, September 13, 2009.

18. Greenleaf, *Servant as Religious Leader,* 34–35.

19. Edgar Schein, *Organizational Culture and Leadership* (San Francisco: Jossey-Bass, 2006), 26.

20. Tom Rath and Barry Conchie, *Strengths Based Leadership* (New York: Gallup, 2008), 88.

21. Malcolm Gladwell, *The Tipping Point* (Boston: Little Brown & Co., 2002), 179.

22. Bass, B. M., and Avolio, B. J. *Improving Organizational Effectiveness through Transformationl Leadership* (Thousand Oaks, CA: Sage, 1994).

23. Thomas Mannarelli, "Accounting for Leadership: Charismatic, Transformational Leadership Through Reflection and Self-awareness," *Accountancy Ireland* 38 (2006): 46–48.

24. Ibid., 47.

25. S. A. Masood et al., "Transformational Leadership and Organizational Culture," *Proceedings of the Institution of Mechanical Engineers* 220 (2006): 941–48.

26. Constant Beugre et al., "Transformational Leadership in Organizations," *International Journal of Manpower* 27 (2006), 55.

27. Bernard Bass and Bruce J. Avolio, *Improving Organizational Effectiveness Through Transformational Leadership* (Thousand Oaks, CA: Sage, 1994).

28. Peter G. Northouse, *Leadership Theory and Practice,* 4th ed. (Thousand Oaks, CA: Sage, 2007), 350.

29. John Wooden, personal communication, February 16, 2007.

30. Jim Collins, *Good to Great* (New York: HarperCollins, 2001), 39.

31. Ibid.

# Chapter Four: Additional Qualities and Traits of Highly Effective Clergy

1. Jim Collins, *Good to Great* (New York: HarperCollins, 2001), 21.

2. Heike Bruch and Sumantra Ghoshal, "Beware the Busy Manager," *Harvard Business Review,* February 2002, 64.

3. Ibid.

4. Jane Creswell, *Coaching for Excellence* (New York: Alpha Books, 2008), 4.

5. Sharon Rhodes-Wickett, personal communication, July 13, 2010.

6. John Southwick, personal communication, January 31, 2011.

7. Jim Griffith, personal communication, May 20, 2005.

8. Malcolm Gladwell, *The Tipping Point* (Boston: LittleBrown&Co., 2002), 166–68.

9. Rosamund Stone Zanders and Benjamin Zander, *The Art of Possibility* (Boston: Penguin, 2002), 110.

10. Ibid.

## Chapter Five: The Critical Role of Church Culture, Systems, and Organizational Development

1. Daniel Goleman, Richard Boyatzis, and Annie McKee, *Primal Leadership: Learning to Lead with Emotional Intelligence* (Cambridge, MA: Harvard Business School Press, 2002), 233–34.

2. Roger Martin, *The Opposable Mind* (Cambridge, MA: Harvard Business School Press, 2007), 93.

3. Ibid., 115–16.

4. Ibid., 147.

5. Ibid., 185–86.

6. Ibid., 186.

7. Linda Moorman, personal communication, November 8, 2011.

8. Marco Cavazzoni, "Evaluating the Impact of Corporate Executive Leadership Programs: Impacts on Executive Behaviors," PhD diss., Pepperdine University, 2002, 171–73.

9. Goleman et al., *Primal Leadership*, 233–34.

10. Edgar Schein, *Organizational Culture and Leadership* (San Francisco: Jossey-Bass, 2002), 26.

11. Ibid.

12. Geert Hofstede et al., "Measuring Organizational Cultures: A Qualitative and Quantitative Study Across Twenty Cases," *Administrative Science Quarterly* 35 (1990), 291.

13. Schein, *Organizational Culture and Leadership*, 291.

14. Ibid., 246.

15. Collins, *Good to Great* (New York: HarperCollins, 2001), 41.